THE POWER OF CONSULTATIVE SELLING

THE POWER OF CONSULTATIVE SELLING

Bryce Webster

Prentice-Hall, Inc.   **Englewood Cliffs, New Jersey**

Prentice-Hall International, Inc., *London*
Prentice-Hall of Australia, Pty. Ltd., *Sydney*
Prentice-Hall Canada, Inc., *Toronto*
Prentice-Hall of India Private Ltd., *New Delhi*
Prentice-Hall of Japan, Inc., *Tokyo*
Prentice-Hall of Southeast Asia Pte. Ltd., *Singapore*
Editora Prentice-Hall do Brasil Ltda., *Rio de Janeiro*
Prentice-Hall Hispanoamericana, S.A., *Mexico*

© 1987 *by*

Bryce Webster

Library of Congress Cataloging-in-Publication Data

Webster, Bryce.
    The power of consultative selling.

    Bibliography: p.
    Includes index.
    1. Selling. 2. Selling—Key accounts. I. Title.
HF5438.25.W287   1987   658.8′1   87-2251

ISBN 0-13-685918-6

ISBN 0-13-686270-5 {PBK}

Printed in the United States of America

To

FRANK MADDEN

Who Led Me Gently Into Consultative Selling,

With Thanks

ACKNOWLEDGMENTS

I owe thanks to hundreds of anonymous salespeople who taught me how rewarding the art and science of selling consultatively can truly be—for both the client and the salesperson.

In any project of this type, many editors and assistants help take the "seed" given them in manuscript form and nurture it until that seed blossoms as a professional book worthy of the Prentice-Hall name. I especially want to thank my editor, Tom Power, for his patience, understanding, professionalism, and good humor.

And, since there are all too many "secret" agents in the literary world, I want to thank mine, Charles Neighbors Jr., without whom this particular garden of prose would not have been planted at all.

WHAT THIS BOOK WILL DO FOR YOU

Gone are the days when sales training consisted of "THE BOSS" telling the salesman to stick his foot in the door to force a prospect to listen to his pitch. It was hard on shoe leather and did a good job of chewing up otherwise excellent salespeople. But more importantly to you, both sellers and buyers of products, from brushes to microcomputers, have gradually become more sophisticated. In fact, many purchasers today, both corporate and consumer, shop for more than a product. Instead, they look for a package of products *and* services, including:

- The product itself
- The product's image
- The image of the company that makes and sells it
- The philosophy underlying both your product and your company's business mission
- The service they can expect once the product is delivered, or, in the case of services,
- How well the service deliverers perform
- The advantages of the product or service including price, naturally, but also possibly design, size, delivery schedule, and so on
- The benefits of the product or service to them, not just directly but indirectly, that is, how well will others think of them for buying it

Of course, even a fast-pitch artist could *tell* a prospect all the information above. But just as customers no longer buy the product "in a vacuum," they don't want to be told. They want to be shown, assured, asked, answered, reassured, respected, served, and then sold. That takes attention to all the factors above, for which your company sets the stage. And it takes attention to these factors, too:

- *Your image*
- *Your attention* to client needs
- *Your sales expertise*
- *Your knowledge of the product,* and, increasingly,
- *Your willingness to work for the buyer* in developing benefits and uses of your product or service

In short, today's corporate buyers expect an awful lot for their money, both from your company and from you. A burdensome responsibility? Not for sales professionals. In fact, it provides you with wider opportunities than any snake oil salesman ever dreamed of. Best of all, providing what your customers want need not cost you a penny, and stands to earn you greater rewards—in income, certainly, but also in expertise, respect, and fulfillment as well.

THE "MAGIC" FORMULA

What is this magic formula? It's no formula at all. It's a technique known as consultative selling. The heart of the consultative, problem-solving approach is two people, salesperson and client, consulting—together—to explore a situation and find a solution. Consultative selling depends not on learning a set of sales pitches, or on being simply a service-minded salesperson, but rather on adding your sales skills and brainpower to those of your prospect to reach a mutually satisfactory result. Successful consultative selling rests, too, upon your own unique power as a salesperson, based on yourself, your company, your product or service, and your clientele. There are, of course, a few basics. But once you're aware of them and have practiced them a few times, you'll find selling more exciting than ever before—and more comfortable as well.

WHERE HAS IT BEEN ALL YOUR LIFE?

Consultative selling, while only lately being applied to commodities from ant traps to training courses, has always been used by some professionals to sell their services. Attorneys, who could not advertise until recently—and then only in limited places with limited impact—have always had to consult with their clients to convince them of the need for their services.

New industries, too, have traditionally had to engage in consultative selling, whether it was called that or not. For example, when today's almost obsolete common business typewriter was invented, selling it required convincing business owners that using it was better than hiring a dozen scribes. It took demonstrating to sell it. It took persistence. It took competitive prices. But most of all, sales forces had to listen to the business owners and come up with ways to fit the new machine to the existing businesses. Today, in the microcomputer business, consultative salespeople do the same thing in selling personal computers, but they call it finding "applications" for the new technology. Then and now, successful selling requires consultative techniques.

THE COMPUTER INDUSTRY EXAMPLE

In the new industry of computing, there has been a tug-of-war in sales techniques. On the one hand, computers are being sold like TVs—in high volume, for cut-rate prices, from warehouse-type outlets, with no sales support or service, let alone presale consultation of any sort. But that market is self-limiting. Only a few buyers are so familiar with these products that they need and want no help. And even fewer are so unsophisticated that they ignore their own lack of knowledge in return for a lower price.

On the other hand, in the corporate computing market, and in many markets where new developments happen daily, the case is much like that of the typewriter's introduction. Prospects do not understand the technology and they tend to be afraid to take the plunge. If you are to sell to them, you first need to discover what objectives a prospect has and what tasks he wants to accomplish. To do this, you'd have to be concerned about the buyer and his situation and truly listen to what he says. You would act as teacher, counselor, guide, consultant, confessor, and often, big brother or sister. Next, you'd need to show the prospect how your products and services could meet or surpass his needs. Finally, you'd need to make sure your company followed through and delivered to the prospect the integrated package of equipment, service, and "consultation" you promised.

The urgent need for consultative selling is apparent in the retail sales of microcomputers, where the successful new breed of computer dealers:

- Take pains to consult with their clients before the purchase
- Hold their clients' hands during the selling process, the negotiations, and both before and after installation
- Continuously follow through, not only with that package, but with consultations about new devices and services which may enhance the buyer's pleasure in the machine or its usefulness

All this takes a particular kind of sales work. You must add to your existing tools—in-depth product knowledge and highly developed sales skills—two new ones: honest curiosity and an ability to be a good audience. You must also be willing to develop and maintain a relationship with a client.

In addition, consultative selling embraces everything you know about yourself, your product, your company, and your client. But it offers you rewards far greater than the one-shot commission, both in terms of money, and of your continued growth in professional and personal satisfaction.

Consultative selling is being developed on two fronts, by the professions and the new industries. Lawyers and accountants have often had no choice but to sell consultatively. They and other professionals were, and in some cases still are, prohibited by law from advertising to gain customers. The new industries, led by computer hardware and software manufacturers, have also chosen, to a great extent, the consultative route, although they are free to advertise and to sell their products any way they please. Traditional industries, too, are using the new techniques effectively, as salespeople have found that their clients need and respond to the same problem-solving approach. Congoleum, a respected manufacturer of a traditional product, floor coverings, has helped lead manufacturing sales out of the dark ages of showmanship into a more enlightened age of problem solving and need fulfillment.

At the end of the book, you will find three original slants on consultative selling: one that has worked almost miraculously for a mature manufacturing company that sells its product to independent retail merchants; one that is working for a new company selling a package of management services to top corporations; and one that's putting a new high-tech company into its precisely targeted market niche, banking and finance, with a new product and a new concept.

Before reviewing these case studies and personal experiences with you, however, *The Power of Consultative Selling* shows how you can make this improved sales concept work.

You'll find that, using the straightforward guidelines found in each chapter, you can add valuable consultative techniques to your sales skills repertoire completely on your own, if need be.

To help you along, this book will first define what consultative selling is, and then quickly and efficiently show you how to become an effective consultative salesperson. Each chapter takes a different aspect of traditional selling—selling skills, probing techniques, closing techniques, and follow-through methods—and "nurtures" it into its expanded consultative role. By practicing these techniques as you work, you will gain the fullest benefits of this book.

Plan to use your new techniques in at least six selling situations within thirty days. By giving yourself hands-on experience, you will reinforce what you've learned, and better still, be able to gauge the rewards of your efforts with the best possible barometers—increased competence, increased enjoyment, and increased income as well.

Bryce Webster

CONTENTS

Chapter 9

Chapter 1

WHAT IS CONSULTATIVE SELLING?

And When Should You Use It?

All selling involves some degree of getting people to do something you want them to do, that is, buy a product or service. It involves some listening, too. You must, for example, take down the order correctly or your "sale" is a return.

THE PURPOSE OF CONSULTATIVE SELLING

Consultative selling goes far beyond the above definition of selling. It means that you must keep in mind not only your own and your company's interests, but your customer's interests as well. In fact, unless you know how to mesh all three complementary needs, you're not selling consultatively. In consultative selling, the product or service you sell is *almost* incidental to the service you provide. And, whether you deliver the product or service as well as sell it (for example, if you are a self-employed management consultant), your sales approach to consultative selling must depend heavily on service. Consultative selling depends on service so heavily, in fact, that you must present yourself not only as the salesperson, but as a serviceperson. You must be aware at all times of all the ways you are "serving." For example, you are:

- *Serving the client's needs,* bringing to him a product or service that he may conceivably want or need; you may even show him this need for the first time.

3

- *Serving as a sounding board* for his problems, but in such a way that you can both empathize with him and suggest solutions.

- *Serving as a finder of solutions* to those problems, and offering alternatives.

- *Serving as a liaison* between your client and your company, to make sure that communication doesn't become garbled.

- *Serving as a troubleshooter* for both your client *and* your company, so that you can sell those of your company's products most suitable to each client's requirements. You can also provide feedback to your company on what your clients are asking for or inquiring about. In this way, you become, also, a valuable market researcher for your company.

- *Serving as an expediter* to see that the client gets his goods or services on time, even if "it's not your job" to check with production.

- *Serving as a matchmaker,* seeing not only that the client gets what he or she wants, but that those desires can be served by your company, and that your company wants the kind of business your customer or potential customer can send its way. For example, in the computer industry, some software houses could serve small, one-person, one-computer offices. But they don't want to. Instead, the corporate mission may be to concentrate on multiunit installations, avoiding the high overhead involved in providing service to tiny outfits. Or, it might be the other way around. In short, keep your company's mission in sight at all times.

- *Serving as a negotiator* for both client and company, so that you can produce not only win-win situations, but win-win-win situations, with yourself included for a blue ribbon.

- *Serving as a researcher* for your client, making sure the client has everything he needs that your company can supply—and nothing he doesn't want or need. You can lead him to complementary services and products that would enhance both your potential sales and his business. Or you could even take a lesson from the movie, *Miracle on 34th Street,* in which the Macy's Santa Claus pointed customers to Gimbels when Macy's didn't have just what was wanted.

THE LANGUAGE OF SUCCESS

To perform all these services, you'll have to learn to be an interpreter, too. Your company may speak one language, and your client another. You'll find, if you examine it, that your own language falls somewhere in between. This is easy to explain. Your company wants sales, preferably big ones for big dollars. Your customer wants purchases, preferably the most product or service for the fewest dollars. You want both. You, too, want big sales for big dollars so you can earn big money. But you also want to please your customer so he or she will return for more. After all, it's easier and usually more profitable for you to continue serving a reliable customer than to continually hunt up new ones to replace those you've lost.

How can you tread these waters? It's easier than you might imagine. Simply run your company's desires through your onboard computer. "Big sale" goes in. You process it. "Best service" comes out, when you think of your approach to your client. And you use those words—the ones your client will respond to—when you present your company's plan for making "Big sales" to him in the form of your product campaign.

Think of another example of the translation you'll have to do, this time in your actions. Your company wants you to succeed. You want to succeed. Your client also wants you to succeed, so you'll continue serving him with good products and services. And that's a relationship to cultivate. He doesn't, however, want you to succeed at his expense. But you *can* succeed at his behest. You can succeed with his cooperation, not through coercion. So be careful not only of what you say, but of how you say it. If your company calls the item you are selling a "Drop-Dead POP Display," be careful not to use that language when you're speaking with someone who would be offended by that common hyperbole; soften it for him. Call it a "Million Dollar Cash-In POP Display," or something likely to mean something to him in the language he speaks. In consultative selling, semantics isn't everything, but it is first among equals.

Is consultative selling just a ten-dollar word for soft soap? Hardly. You could make soap out of snake oil.

Is consultative selling giving away your expertise with no hope of return, because it is "tacky" to ask for the order? Not at all. Neither you nor your company could survive that way, nor could your clients. They have legitimate requirements, and someone is going to serve them. In a consultative selling relationship, the buyer will expect to be asked to buy, and you certainly have more than one obligation to ask for the sale.

Is consultative selling telling a client what he or she should do and then making sure it gets done? No. Heavy-handedness has no place in consultative selling. Overbearing and pushy salespeople are, more and more often, seen not as experts, but as boors acting more impolitely than anyone expects—or will tolerate.

Consultative selling is not, in fact, a single concept, but a combination of a number of interesting and often delightful ones, brought together to make sense—and dollars—out of the intrinsically adversarial art of selling. Consultative selling is:

- *Knowing your products or services*—inside and out
- *Knowing yourself*—and using your strengths to perform well for your company, yourself, and your client
- *Knowing your client*—what his or her needs and wants are, what his or her biases are, what his or her strengths and weaknesses are, and understanding all of these
- *Knowing how to present your product, your self-knowledge, and your client knowledge*—in an intelligent package, not a slick and perfect "canned" one, to best fulfill the interests of all concerned

ALMOST EVERYONE CAN JOIN THE SALES TEAM

Outside salespeople most certainly can benefit from using consultative selling, but inside salespeople can, too. Often, in fact, clients and customers say things—give hints about their needs—over the telephone that they might not say in person. Whether the telephone salesperson uses the information directly, or passes it on after giving a consultative response to the appropriate account representative, it becomes part of the consultative selling effort. Even non-salespeople can use consultative selling techniques. A client might offhandedly tell your billing department something of value to the sales force; the billing clerk—and all others who ever contact clients directly—should be made aware of consultative selling techniques and urged to use them when appropriate. The clerk should also pass the customer on to a sales professional who can follow up.

WHEN IS CONSULTATIVE SELLING USEFUL?

It would be a snap to say "all the time." And that's both true and untrue. It's untrue if you unthinkingly suggest additional purchases at every chance or planned meeting with a client. If you appear to push products or services at the drop of a hat, the client will begin to feel like your personal Golden Goose. That's insulting at best, and counterproductive at worst. As a consultative specialist, there are times when you will choose to act merely as an order-taker for current purchases.

Because consultative selling has to do with more than just talk about your product or service, you can still use even an order-taking encounter to "consult" with your client—about the future of widgets, the short- and long-term directions of both companies, his or her department's changing needs, new or revised training techniques and courses. You may choose not to mention the Mighty Moe Wrench you know they can sell—

this time. You may feel as if you've wasted a golden opportunity to ask for an order. But you will be building a reputation as a consultant as well as a sales rep. In today's business atmosphere, in which conduct, add-ons, and perceptions of value often make the difference when price and quality don't, it will end up being time well and profitably spent. In future chapters, you'll see just how.

Chapter 2

KNOW YOUR PRODUCT

The Mind of Consultative Selling

Before you can sell anything, you must be able to make a coherent presentation, first to yourself, and then to the client. In consultative selling the presentation is doubly important and includes far more ways to present your product and yourself than traditional selling ever did. In today's market, if you're selling a tangible such as machine tools or roller skates, you already have a lot of competition. In intangibles, from financial services to educational consulting, you've got increasingly stiff competition, naturally, and you've also got the competition of ignorance. Many current or potential clients will be unfamiliar with what your untouchable, unseeable product does, and, more importantly, what benefits it will bring them. In both cases, you've got to begin your presentation with product knowledge.

HAVE IN-DEPTH PRODUCT KNOWLEDGE

In consultative selling, simply knowing the configuration of your product or service won't do. You've got to know, in depth, abundant facts about your product, its uses, its origin, and its future. Your background knowledge should be extensive, including these sorts of information:

• **Technical.** Knowing that a computer's internal processor operates at four megahertz is technical knowledge. That sort of knowledge is germane to a selling situation—but only if it is backed by the following kinds of knowledge.

• **Hypothetical.** Knowing that a computer *could* process up to 5,000 accounts per hour is hypothetical or theoretical product knowledge. It, too, has little meaning for you or a customer without further information, particularly information about a customer's needs. Perhaps a customer does not want to process accounts at all; mentioning that the machine processes accounts could confuse this customer. Still, it is knowledge you may well need for a different customer. You need not trot out all your knowledge at once. Choose your subject to set off the rest of your presentation properly and appropriately.

• **Promotional.** Offering a special 25-percent-off sale on this computer for the next thirty days may be helpful, but you still do not know whether the customer needs a computer, what he needs it for, what features and benefits are most important, and more.

• **Customer-oriented information.** This is the key category of information any consultative salesperson must have. By having this information, you can shape the other types of information into a form that directly satisfies your needs, your company's mission, and your customer's desires. A prerequisite is knowing the fundamental technical and hypothetical information, the characteristics your products share with competing ones, and the promotional avenues you can follow. Once you know these features, you achieve customer-oriented knowledge by adding to them the advantages and potential benefits of the product or service to all your current and potential customers.

CREATE PROFILES OF YOUR PRODUCTS

How do you obtain this customer-oriented information? In many cases, your company or, if you are a distributor, the manufacturer provides adequate information on how customers can use your product or service, and what benefits they may gain. Often, this information is not conveniently available, or it may not reflect your own experience or the experience of field salespeople or customers themselves.

A classic example of a product languishing for years because no one knew the customer-oriented information is that of 3M's Post-It™ notes. For a long time, the 3M staff had used the notes for their own convenience. After many years, one bright person suggested that if the stick-ems were so popular at 3M, other office workers might pay to use them. And thus, after the usual months of wrangling and planning, a significant new office product was born. Before the potential was explored, 3M sales and marketing people had overlooked the *benefits* of the stick-em notes, rejecting the product on the basis of its unexciting features—tiny scraps of perfect-bound paper.

You, too, may be overlooking similar benefits intrinsic in the products or services your company already markets. To find them, so you can market them, begin with the first item on the product/service agenda, its features. A feature is simply a description of your product. For example, the fact that a machine lathe operates at a speed of 5,000 rpms is a feature.

An advantage is what your product does that others do not. For example, your 5,000-rpm machine forms steel tubing 50 percent faster with 10 percent less waste than a 2,500-rpm machine.

But the benefit is the improvement the product brings for the customer: the 5,000-rpm lathe reduces labor costs by 15 percent, costs the same as the slower, older model, and according to quality testing, saves 33 percent of the maintenance cost of the older model.

If these types of information for your company's products are not readily available from your company or its suppliers, make two sets of charts or *product profiles* for your offerings. First, write up a comprehensive chart for each product or service, containing the twenty-six types of information given below.

Each profile will be more detailed, if you do it right, than your company's product brochure. You need not, in most cases, have the in-depth knowledge of a service technician, although there are exceptions to this rule in technical selling when field sales engineers also sell.

Figure 2–1 gives twenty-six recommended information categories for a complete product profile.

Figure 2–1

PRODUCT PROFILE INFORMATION CATEGORIES

1. Basic product description.
2. Product features and advantages.
3. Potential benefits to customers.
4. Potential customers and precall qualifications.
5. Likely customer contact: purchasing agent, department manager, office manager, comptroller.
6. Likely customers: Who may be interested in this product?
7. Successful case history to relate to customer.
8. Competitive products.
9. Product comparison with competition's products.
10. Probing, need-seeking questions
11. Possible objections and responses.
12. Your responses to objections.
13. Possible closes.
14. Delivery schedules/implementation steps.
15. Prices and terms.
16. Current discounts, special promotions.
17. Company contact for technical backup.
18. Starting dates/delivery dates.
19. Contracts/agreements/required paperwork.
20. Service contracts.
21. Long-term sales possibilities.
22. Cross-selling alert: related products and services to offer.
23. Product family related to various benefits.
24. Brochures, sales aids, exhibits available.
25. Customer feedback.
26. Product summary.

Your company can easily offer hundreds of products, especially if you sell through catalogs, so compiling such an extensive profile of each product would take far too much time. In that case, compile detailed profiles like the one in Figure 2–1 only for product families, and use the chart in Figure 2–2 for the major products or services in your line.

A F/A/B-ulous Chart

This smaller chart should revolve around just three categories: features, advantages, benefits. Figure 2–2 gives a short

Figure 2–2

SAMPLE F/A/B CHART FOR EXECUTIVE RETREAT
FEATURE—ADVANTAGE—BENEFIT

Feature: What is the product or service?

"Exclusive executive retreat located on 500-acre lake in Blue Ridge Mountains. Full-purpose retreat with complete conferencing facilities, year-round recreational activities, and up-to-date communications and computing systems."

Advantage: What does this retreat do?

"Allows participants in company meetings, sales conferences, executive strategy sessions, to get away from distractions of office and family. Gives meeting leaders the audience's undivided attention. Provides chance to combine intense conference sessions with team recreation to reinforce company loyalty among participants."

Benefit: What is in it for me, the buyer?

"You won't lose participants to the attractions of a city. You can control attendance and shorten time spent on conferences, yet make more efficient use of that time, spreading work sessions throughout morning, afternoon, and evening hours. All this at a cost far less than the cost of a less complete facility near company headquarters."

---

example of a chart for a company that owns a mountain retreat and rents it for executive conferences.

Create a similar simple chart for every major product or
service you sell. When you've done that, you'll have a coherent
basis for working up a *consultation protocol* that will allow you
to pick and choose those items you believe will best appeal to
each client. Constructing and using a *consultation protocol* will
be explained in Chapter 3.

Make sure you use your own language in working up
these charts, replacing words—unless they are trademarks or
in other ways critical—that your company uses if these words
are not comfortable for you or your customer. Company literature may, at times, be filled with jargon that your customers
do not understand. But unless you've prepared, or purchased,
professional-looking visual aids, do not show the charts to
clients. They are your "homework," and that's what they
should remain.

TRACK YOUR COMPETITION

Once you have established a system for keeping on top of
information about your own company's products, you need to
know about your competitor's products as well. Of course,
knowing the competition is fundamental to almost every
salesperson, but it becomes particularly important in consultative selling. The key to the consultative approach is to discover customers' needs, requirements, and problems, and
provide solutions and fulfillment. Often, you may find your
own products do not completely solve a problem. Instead of
letting a sale slip away, a consultative salesperson would
know a product or service that would complement his own,
even if that product were made by a competitor. With the
combination, he could recommend a complete solution instead
of either a partial one or none at all.

And, of course, you need competitive information so you can emphasize your own products' advantages and benefits compared with and contrasted to those of competitors. Consultative salespeople in industrial and commercial sales often find, too, that experienced buyers have a thorough knowledge of the products offered by their principal competitors. And buyers often test salespeople to find out how deep their competitive product knowledge is. If you do not have broad knowledge of your competition's major lines and in-depth knowledge of their directly competitive products, your customers may think you shallow or ignorant. You may also "fall for" customer comments about competitive offers ("XYZ company says it will give me a 15 percent discount") or rumors of competitors' advantages or "new" products ("I believe I heard XYZ is about to introduce a new gizmo with more horsepower than your gizmo"). You must know if the information is true or is likely to be true, or is simply the price-beating ploy of a seasoned purchaser.

So, you must remain well-informed about your competition, and have with you brief, but accurate, comparisons of the principal competition's strengths and weaknesses and your products' best selling points. Again, prepare charts, for yourself, as homework. Figure 2–3 shows a simple chart contrasting the competitive services of two local banks.

You can create such charts for each competitor or an overall chart for all principal competitors. These charts could also be turned into customer handouts or professionally prepared visual aids to use during your personal presentations.

You may find it difficult to find competitive information in some fields, especially when you sell new or unique products, or make sales pitches to clients for products or services under development. You may not be able to find out exactly how the competition is responding or plans to respond, but you can form objective opinions based on your previous experience with the competition.

Figure 2-3

COMPETITIVE BANKING SERVICE COMPARISON		
Competition's Strengths	**Competition's Weaknesses**	**Our Selling Advantages**
Numerous branches	Short hours	Early hours, ATM's, Saturday hours
High-interest CD's	High minimums	No-minimum money market/checking accounts
Low mortgage rates	20% down payment requirement	95% mortgages, variable rates, flexible payments
Low personal loan rates	No credit card services	Visa/MasterCard services; quick loan processing

BE A "FUTURIST" FOR YOUR CLIENTS: TELL THEM WHAT'S AHEAD

It is also essential for you to understand the general history, development, and trends of your own business or industry and those of your clients, even if they are consumers and not commercial customers. Clients want to keep up with the times, stay in fashion, or be "with it," even if they don't intend to wear punk hairdos and dress in quilted bedsheets or leather pants. If they've contacted you for a sales presentation, or have allowed you to give them one, they probably have a business or personal need to know the latest trends in your field, and you can perform a valuable service by helping them keep informed. If you sell life insurance, consumers will want to know what universal life is all about; if you sell personal computers, they'll want to know what impact the new laser storage disks will have on their current and future purchases, and so forth.

In short, being a consultative salesperson means acting as a client's *personal expert,* someone he believes will always be on top of the situation as that situation affects your market, industry, company, and products. And, of course, the client's own situation.

How do you obtain and maintain such knowledge? By constant study of trade journals and publications aimed at your own and your customers' industries. If you are in consumer sales, keep track of consumer publications aimed at your markets. For example, if you sell designer dresses, you will, of course, read *Women's Wear Daily* for industry information. But also read *Town & Country, Vogue,* and other popular magazines that carry fashion ads and articles to know what your upscale customers are likely to be thinking about—whether they are aware of it or not. Read *Mademoiselle* and *Seventeen* for insight into the desires of your more youthful clients.

If you are in commercial or industrial sales, use your customer's knowledge and the information available about his company to support your own reasearch. Scan your client's own product literature. Read his company's annual reports, in-house literature, and so forth. Use your sales calls, when possible, to talk to support personnel, visit factories and facilities, and observe the client's business environment not only to find out what and how he is doing, but to add to your overall knowledge of industry conditions.

If your presales-call study does not yield all the information you need about a client's line of business and needs, you will have to ask him the necessary questions. Chapter 4 will discuss a variety of probing questions and techniques you can use.

CUSTOMIZE YOUR PRESENTATION

Presentations in consultative selling differ from those in traditional selling. In a traditional presentation you do a lot of talking as you try to convince the prospect your product is superior to others. The client's situation or problem is secondary. In consultative selling, the reverse is true: the client's situation is paramount, and your presentation is designed to elicit how your product or service can solve that problem. You will structure it so that your client has plenty of time to do lots of talking. Exactly how you elicit the responses you need will be dealt with later on. First, however, you've got to learn how to organize your active part of the presentation.

The key words are *plan and practice*. To plan your presentation, you will need to use the information in Chapter 3, "Know Your Client," to develop a business and psychological profile of your client and his company. Once you have a thorough knowledge of your own products and of the client's company, you can develop a presentation that integrates your spoken message with selected visual or sales aids and, at the same time, stays on target for the client's probable concerns.

Following are the basic components and steps to take in preparing your consultative presentation.

POLISH YOUR USE OF VISUAL AIDS

If your company provides visual aids for your presentations, from brochures to films, it's essential that you become familiar not only with their content, but also with the *mechanics* of their use. Run through a slide show for peers first. If you're all thumbs around electronic equipment, get a wizard to design a foolproof way for you to handle it. If a particular sales aid is a sales disaster in your hands, attempt to get permission to substitute something more amenable to you. Failing that, accept your shortcomings, apologize simply, and get on with the portions of your total presentation—your consultation package—that you can handle like the pro you are.

ADD HUMOR, BUT WITH A MESSAGE

Next, add spice and color to your presentation. Use anecdotes, humorous stories (but not off-color jokes), and testimonials to boost the impact of your message.

Let's assume that you sell a package of sales training tools and that package can generate, on average, an increase of 15 percent in call-backs for the companies who buy your service. You can just tell the client that, and leave it as a dry statistic. Or, you can follow it with a nonjudgmental, true, and entertaining anecdote, to help it stick in the client's mind and to make your message more valuable to the client. Here's an example:

"Company X was very much a result-driven company, but management realized it had a problem. One of its salesmen got call-backs on fully 90 percent of the cold canvassing he did. His office partner, however, got absolutely none. The manager didn't want to fire the man without another try. So, he contracted for our training. The super salesman, needless to say, didn't go up to 105 percent. He stayed about the same. But the other man increased his sales call-backs to 30 percent, which was just about the norm in that field. The average for the two men was 60 percent, twice the average, making a happy ending for both of them. Especially since salesman number two was the owner's son."

This anecdote combines product information, advantages, direct benefits to the client (most companies have a salesperson with a low rate of call-backs), and humor. The humorous twist at the end helps make the story—and the message that the client will receive psychological satisfaction from your product—stick in the client's mind.

Most salespeople know a wealth of jokes and funny stories, and these have long been used to make friends with or "soften up" a client. However, not many salespeople use their jokes or humorous stories to increase the psychological impact of the product in the client's mind. Too often, jokes and anecdotes only result in creating a lasting impression of the *salesperson,* not of what he is selling. Change that impact, using humor to drive home the benefits a client can expect from your product, and you will probably increase repeat sales.

USE VIDEO, AND PRECISE PREPARATION, TO SHARPEN YOUR IMAGE

With low cost video equipment readily available from your company or for rental or purchase at any discount appliance store, you can get added mileage from practicing your presentations "live."

Write out your presentation beforehand, and edit and re-edit until you have condensed it to the appropriate length. In the first version, throw in everything—every fact, every point, every benefit you can imagine. Then, cut out all of the unnecessary facts, points, or benefits, or those that do not concern a particular customer. By the time you finish editing, your *core presentation* should be no more than one to three minutes long.

Like a story, a movie, or a novel, your presentation should have a beginning (also called an opening), a middle, and an end. Your product or service and how it benefits the client will be the theme. Always begin a presentation with a *grabber,* preferably a humorous story or point directly related to your theme. Then, with humor added as a sprinkling of spice, explain the benefits your client will receive—emotional as well as business—and close with a quick summary. Remember to *always* ask for the order. Chapter 7 explains many types of consultative closing techniques, but the key is, of course, to *always ask for the sale.* Even the most favorably disposed buyer wants to be asked to buy, and, if you think about it, asking someone to buy becomes an act of great courtesy.

In making your presentation, make sure you:

- Are appropriately dressed.
- Have marshalled all your information and have either stored it in your mental computer for reference or included it in your speech.
- Have your voice and speech patterns under control.
- Have your body language well in hand.

In making first or formal presentations, there are a few physical habits that are all-too-easy traps to fall into. Here are tips to help you avoid throwing unconscious curves into your own presentation:

• Do not blink your eyes excessively; this implies nervousness or shiftiness to a client.

• Do not nod or wiggle your head. Keep your head firmly, but not stiffly, straight.

• Do not use broad or histrionic gestures more appropriate to nineteenth century orators in Congress. But don't sit on your hands, either.

• Do not swallow too hard, so that your Adam's Apple bounces up and down.

• Make sure you use the proper terms and know how to pronounce any foreign phrases you use, *savoir-faire, joie de vivre,* etc.

• Do not slur any word pronunciations. Speak clearly. Slow down your rate of speech slightly to make sure you pronounce every word clearly.

• Do not look down. Look at your client and make frequent eye contact without staring. Look down only when drawing a client's attention to a sales aid or a contract.

• Look pleased and enthusiastic, as if you are enjoying yourself. Do not look too serious, unless you are selling something so stupendously serious that it will eliminate disease or bring peace on earth.

• Plant your feet firmly on the floor whether standing or sitting.

• Do not point to your mouth or cheekbones, don't tug your hair, don't bite your nails, scratch your head, etc. In short, avoid nervous gestures.

• Change your facial expressions; let your facial muscles relax now and then so you will not appear to be locked into a fixed grin or worse, a scowl.

• Let your shoulders relax, but keep an erect posture.

• Transfer your enthusiasm to the buyer. Show the "glamour" or the "aura" of being associated with your product.

• Watch for the client's reactions—facial expressions, shifts in position, body language, and emotional reactions you can feel—and act (not react) to get them more in line with yours.

• Above all, remember to *listen* for buying signals. And act on them immediately. Do not "save" buying signals to the end of a presentation; stop your pitch and move directly to probing questions that lead directly to closing questions and a formal close.

• Get the client or buyer involved in your presentation. Make him a straight man for your jokes. Ask questions for factual information. Encourage clients to conjure up mental pictures of the benefits you describe. Lead them to experience emotional reactions to what you are saying. In short, help them invest themselves in your presentation.

PREPARE YOUR CLIENT FOR THE CLOSE

Even after you make your presentation—after you have worked through a client's objections and have moved toward the close—you have not yet finished presenting yourself. Your presentation at the actual moment of signing a contract remains essential to the deal. As a very famous negotiator once told me: "No deal is ever finished until money changes hands." So, if you close the sale rudely or obnoxiously, you may find the client will back out at the last second or arrange to kill the deal at a later stage of review. And no money will change hands. No sale.

Be sure to graciously and professionally close each sale or agreement. Some of the best lawyers, negotiators, and sales professionals know that they can lose ground—if not the sale—by forcing contracts on a client too soon. Popping a contract out of your briefcase at the moment of signing can be startling too, and scare a client into forgetting everything you've been talking about. A good tactic is to leave a contract inconspicuously on your lap or desk; the client will know it's there and won't be nearly as threatened when you pass it to him for review and signature.

SAY "THANK YOU"

In closing the sale, you lay the groundwork for the next sales call. Always leave the customer with a polite, firm, but not groveling or gratuitous ("Oh, thank you for the sale, now I can get braces for my kids") thank you. Make sure the client knows he can always contact you in case he has more questions or runs into difficulties.

In consultative selling more than in any other type of sales, you are the client's liaison with your company. You act as the "point guard" for your client's interests with your company. Let the client know this at the close of every sale. And, if you make frequent sales calls (once a month or more often), use the end of the sales call to make an appointment for the next one.

In addition, some companies have policies and procedures in place for thanking their valued clients. Yours may. Take advantage of it. But add your own personal thanks as well. Attorneys often present a bill showing a charge "minus courtesy," sometimes as much as 5 percent of the bill, for clients they know well. You may not have such leeway.

But it will cost you little and be worth much to invest in some personal business stationery suitable for sending a short note of thanks—or a clipping you see that will interest your client, or a congratulatory note on their son's graduation, anything to enhance the client's positive impression of you, and positive feelings about himself. In consultative selling, absence does not make the heart grow fonder.

For example, a very successful packaging consultant, who helped corporations design their bags, packages, and containers, spent much of his time flying from city to city. Instead of sleeping or reading in-flight magazines, he used his air time to write thank you notes, and find clippings in trade journals that either mentioned a client by name (such as announcement of a promotion, involvement in an industry conference, or a leading position in a company) or told about a positive development (such as record sales or new acquisitions) by a client's company. He would tear out the clipping, write a brief note of congratulations on the clipping itself, and put it in a small, personalized envelope with a business card. He addressed and stamped the envelope on the spot and put it in the mail as soon as he landed.

This expert told me that no amount of paid advertising, nor any number of hired public relations hands could compare to the amount of business he gained—and kept—by sending those notes. He had too many clients to keep track of their birthdays and their children's birthdays, and he knew that they would be more impressed when he reinforced or evoked once again the good feelings they felt when something good happened to them or their company.

BLOW YOUR OWN HORN, BUT WISELY

In consultative selling, then, the job doesn't end when you've got the agreement to purchase. It continues into the building of a relationship. It may even go beyond that, if you like, into further establishing your own expertise. How? By using business and personal public relations.

Of course, your company will do its own public relations, and you can use much of this to build your own public image; with one hand continually washing the other, both come out smelling like roses. If your company is mentioned prominently in a newspaper or magazine—*and the mention has interest for a specific client*—send it along with a cheery FYI note.

You can help your professional standing, enhance your expertise and the perception of your expertise by indulging in personal public relations when the chance arises. It's not blowing your own horn, if you're asked to speak at a local college about your industry, to invite one of your clients who might be interested. If you contribute an article to a journal—and it is of interest to your client, or pertinent to a project you've got underway together—send it along.

The rule of thumb is this: If it's pertinent, positive, and interesting, it's public relations and has value to both of you. If it's not pertinent, is unflattering, or sounds downright dull— you're blowing your own horn.

Conclusion? In consultative selling, your presentation is not just what you set before your client in a meeting. It begins before that with your ability to work up a three-pronged presentation of your product or service, incorporating features, advantages, and benefits. During the sales sessions, your presentation will depend on what you've done about *you*—your attention to mannerism, speech, dress, etiquette. It will continue after the sale, not only when you carry out product- or service-specific contact with the client, but when you let him know that you are generally keeping his needs in mind. And it can extend beyond that, to using business and personal public relations to enhance your expertise, your company and personal image, and your current clients'—and future clients'— trust in you.

Chapter 3

KNOW YOUR CLIENT

The Heart of Consultative Selling

Once you know how to make presentations to clients, concentrate on understanding who your client is and what he or she wants and needs. To do this, you will have to find and examine several levels of information about your clients and their companies. Information is arranged in layers, from the superficial (obvious information concerning the client's name, position, etc.) to the psychological (his emotional motivation and even the group psychology of the client's company). To round up the information, you'll have to look diligently, peeling away each layer of the information onion. Later, you can use your customary analytical skills (plus some more hints given in later chapters) to reorganize the information so that you can use it to serve your client well.

Here's an example of how one such "information onion" might be peeled.

Let's say that you sell teddy bears, among other toy and gift items. A consumer comes into your store to look at your stock. On a superficial level, you would probably quickly find out that the consumer has a teddy bear collection. You want to encourage him to add to it, so you might point out your most unusual bear, a fierce polar bear made of Alaskan stone.

But, if you probed further, you'd find out he doesn't collect bears for their antique or collectible value, but because he feels emotionally attached to teddy bears. They make him feel warm and loving and loved. At first, you are amazed because

31

this customer is a huge, burly, scowly man. In fact, he resembles a grizzly. You can't simply ask him if he sleeps with a teddy bear (although, it turns out, he does.) He probably won't reveal to a stranger, which you are at this point, that he was an orphan and his bear was his only attachment to home. But, if you are sufficiently genuinely curious, he might sooner or later tell you, "No, we don't collect antique ones; we just really like teddy bears." Over time, maybe not today but as your relationship builds, he might tell you the full reason for his attachment to the bears. But meanwhile, you will have developed enough information to decide to shift your focus from the stone or antique or costly bears to soft, cuddly ones with charming facial expressions.

This psychological approach works throughout all aspects of consumer sales. Why else do consumer product companies put women's deodorants in pinks and pastel packaging? Or make women's razors in pink with soft, rounded shapes, and men's razors sharp-edged in deep masculine colors? This approach also works in commercial and industrial sales far more often than one might think—although purchasing agents and buyers tend to disguise their psychological motivation behind business terminology.

With careful attention to building your knowledge from the most to the least apparent, you can discover these motivations and use them to create winning situations all around.

GET THE FACTS BEFORE YOU SELL: DEVELOP CUSTOMER PROFILES

BASIC COMPANY PROFILE

The first level of information you acquire should be superficial knowledge: the readily available basics of any company and the buyer or client. *Before* a sales call or interview, find answers to the questions below:

• *What is the company's (or division's or unit's) line of business:* wholesale, retail, manufacturing, professional practice, nonprofit organization, small business, etc.?

• *Who is the highest ranking manager or executive with whom you are likely to deal?* In insurance sales, this might be a comptroller or risk management vice-president; in banking, it should be a chief financial officer or comptroller; in manufacturing, it should be the CEO; in retail sales, it might be the head buyer or vice-president of sales; etc.

• *Who are the clients or buyers to whom you are most likely to sell directly?* Buyer, purchasing agent, purchasing manager, purchasing vice-president, department head, office manager, president of the company (in small businesses), VP-manufacturing, a buying committee or team, etc.?

• *Very importantly, which of these individuals makes the final buying decision?* Remember always to get to the decisionmaker as soon as possible, even if you have to arrange a meeting between your sales vice-president and the client's vice-president of purchasing. Meeting repeatedly with buyers with no final authority is a waste of valuable time. You also need to know that many middle-range staffers tend to pretend to have buying authority when they don't. The quickest way to separate the wheat from the chaff is with a simple, polite question: Do you have the final authority to make this purchase? Most people will then tell you directly their position. If the answer is yes, proceed. If it is no, you still have to sell this buyer—even more so—to enlist his aid in helping you sell the decisionmaker.

• *How long has the company been in business?*

• *What is the company's sales volume (or consumer's income level), number of employees, net worth, number of factories, etc.?*

• *With what type of office are you dealing?* Headquarters, subsidiary office, plant office, sales office? Do the personnel at this office have buying authority?

• *What is the client's reputation in its industry, with its customers, with its competition?* You can find this out by asking competitors, customers, and industry officials.

• *What is the client's current relationship with your own company, if any?* Is this a good customer of long standing, occasional customer, customer in arrears, former customer? If your prospect is a former customer, why did they stop doing business with your firm? You'll have to carefully probe your own sales management and other salespeople to find out the whole story. Unless you do, you might fall into a messy stew like the following.

A new advertising salesman for a small town paper approached a local herb farm about a combined advertising purchase with publication of a short article about the farm. The herb farm sales manager loved the idea, and agreed to do it.

The new ad salesman proudly returned to his office with the good news, only to face a very angry assistant sales manager. "How could you do that?" he screamed. "They still owe us $665 from ads they ran four months ago."

What happened? The new salesman failed to ask for the most available information of all, information his own company could provide, concerning the background of this account. If he had, he still might have been able to sell the ads, but with a happier ending. He might have bundled the new ads into payment for the old ones. At the very least, he might have reconsidered twisting the news department's arm to do a costly article until after the account had been paid in full. He could even have used the prospect of an article as a lever for payment and future sales.

• *What are the client's known or stated goals and objectives,* overall, and in dealing with your company? Overall goals are often found in annual reports and similar publications. What they want from you may be known by the experience others in your firm have had with them.

• *What factors restrain your client from buying from you?* Could it be because of budget, poor revenues, competition, having an established product line already in place? This is a very real problem for competitors in the computer industry where most corporations use IBM mainframes. It forces competition to make IBM-compatible products if they want to penetrate other segments of that market, thus limiting both their own design efforts and sales efforts as well. When items are virtually the same across many manufacturers, the primary place you have left to deal is price, or possibly service.

• *Have you been or can you be referred to the client by a third party the client trusts?* In any type of selling, word-of-mouth always has been and always will be the best advertising and often the best credentials.

• *What problems, concerns, and requirements does your client have?* This question begins to unpeel a deeper level of client knowledge.

DETAILED BUYER PROFILE

In addition to information about the company, you need to know about the person (or people) with whom you will deal directly. This information will not be publicly available and may have to be carefully elicited during your first several sales calls.

Here are key questions about individual buyers you need to answer as you develop a customer profile:

• *What is the person's age, sex, title, position, experience, or years with his or her company?*

• *Who are the person's direct superiors?*

• *What is the person's buying authority?* For example, most organizations allow buyers to approve purchases up to certain price levels. More expensive purchases have to be kicked to the next or higher levels in the hierarchy or be considered by a buying committee. To exaggerate, if you sell erasers, you will sell to low level buyers; if you sell office automation systems, you will sell to a large buying team, and can expect months of meetings, demonstrations, pilot programs, and sales calls before a major sale is finalized.

• *What does the person's personal style appear to be?* Conservative, flamboyant, casual, trendy, middle-class, blue-collar? You can ask others in your company who have worked with this person.

• *What is the person's reputation in the industry?* Hardnosed or cooperative?

• *On what points does he or she tend to concentrate?* Facts about products and technology, benefits to the company, savings in dollars to the company, benefits to his or her career or position, etc.

• *What are the buyer's obvious goals and objectives, as they relate to the company's?*

• *What are the buyer's personal goals and objectives in terms of career, lifestyle, family, relationship to superiors, etc.?*

• *What has been the person's relationship with your own company?* Good, so-so, or do you need to mend a lot of fences?

• *Can you obtain a positive referral to this person from another client or someone else in the industry whom you can trust?*

ANALYZE YOUR CUSTOMER PROFILES

Gather as much information about all your clients and their companies as you feasibly can. In retail selling and in making cold calls, this may be difficult, but not impossible. Carefully maintain and update your profile of each customer. Over time, and with simple questioning techniques, you will be able to determine who your average customers are, what their psychographics and demographics are, and what motivates them to buy.

Take, for example, the practice of an author who specializes in the production and packaging of crafts books. For fifteen years, she has successfully written, edited, and prepared for publication books about home crafts—crocheting, needle-work, and the like. In the beginning, she developed book ideas as most authors do—by hit or miss. But as she prospered, she began to notice patterns: some books did better than others, books sold better at certain times of the year and so forth. Her publisher urged her to regularize their arrangement and work on long-term contracts. She then realized that to maximize her book sales, and smooth out the peaks and valleys in her income, she needed to know a lot more about her audience: who bought her books, when, where, and why. So, she began to ask them, through mailed questionnaires, at book-signing parties, seminars and conferences, wherever she was. Today, she has a computerized profile of her customer bases, and she can tell any publisher the exact demographics of her average customer, what kind of books they will buy, at what time of year, how much they will pay for each book, and how many they will buy over the course of several years.

ASSEMBLE "QUICKY" PROFILES

Using simple, short statements you, too, can quickly assemble a profile of your average customer, whether you work in consumer or commercial sales. In retail selling, an astute salesperson can gain, in months, the equivalent of years of experience by jotting down a quick customer profile on 3-x-5-inch notecards, after each sale or during breaks in the action. A sample customer notecard for a cosmetics salesperson might include:

> "Jan. 15, 1987. First-time customer. Woman, 35–40 years old, well-dressed, but preppy style. Bought $25 worth of moisturizer, hand creams, all Crabtree & Evelyn. Used American Express. Expressed fondness for English-style toiletries and perfumes with light floral fragrances. Name: Mrs. Ashley Farnsworth, 1515 Tory Hill Lane, Shaker Heights, OH."

Obviously, you can develop your own shorthand to make writing these notes much faster. An occasional quick review of such notes will implant the customer's name and preferences in your mind. Reviewing all your cards occasionally will reveal buying patterns to you much faster and more accurately than relying on memory alone.

USE THE CONSULTATION PROTOCOL

As you gather detailed client knowledge, combine that knowledge with your knowledge of yourself and your own products. Use the combination to create a Consultation Protocol. Simply put, a consultation protocol is a method by which you can match your products and services with your customer's emotional and business needs. Let's construct a simple consultation protocol for the man buying a teddy bear.

TEDDY BEAR PROTOCOL

Teddy Bear Product Knowledge:

In stock, you have:

- –Carved stone bears
- –Antique teddy bears, true collectibles
- –Stuffed, cuddly teddy bears, in many colors, sizes, styles
- –Character bears, such as Muffy vander Bear, Humphrey Beargart and so on
- –Mechanical, robotic, and talking bears
- –Teddy bear greeting cards and gifts
- –Teddy bear coffee mugs

Teddy Bear Customer Knowledge:

- –Adults buy for themselves or their spouses as gifts
- –Buyers tend to own lots of teddy bear-type things

–Buyers tend to be susceptible to add-on sales

–Adults buy for children mostly at Christmas or birthdays

–Adults tend to hate talking bears, prefer cuddly ones with cute, often period clothing

–Men bear buyers tend to be slightly embarrassed

–If men know what they want, they tend to ask for it right away

–Women teddy bear buyers tend to know generally what they want, but want you to ask them what it is and show them specifically what you have, in case there's something they haven't thought of

–Average buyers spend $20–$25 per bear

–The average teddy bear purchase is a small, six- to ten-inch tall soft, cuddly-style bear

MAKE EDUCATED GUESSES

From the example at the first of this chapter, you know the customer is a large, burly, grizzly male, who buys teddy bears he likes, not antique or true collectible bears. He is buying for himself or his spouse, since he has on a wedding ring. As a haphazard collector, he may be susceptible, you think, to impulse buying of additional teddy bear items.

You don't know and you can't ask, but you can guess that the customer is in his late thirties, holds a professional or executive position, and dresses well, but slightly conservatively. It appears he is browsing and does not have any particular bear in mind. He may be able to spend more than the average on a teddy bear.

THE F/A/B SALES APPROACH

Now, you can ask more probing questions to find out what the customer wants, that is, what emotional pleasure he wants to receive by buying the bear. For example, is he looking for a gift or something for himself? He says he is buying a gift for his spouse. You can assume he wants the emotional satisfaction of buying a nice present for his spouse and the warmth and affection she will give him when she receives the present. Then, follow the F/A/B (Features–Advantages–Benefits) approach to fulfill that need.

You decide to present to the customer a fairly large, perhaps very femininely outfitted, but very soft and cuddly bear. These are its features. It could even have hearts or flowers or romantic sentiments with it. Since it is a gift, it could easily be somewhat more expensive than average, and you could offer to gift wrap it for the buyer. Its advantages would be that its romantic or sentimental expression accentuates the giving of a gift. Its benefits would be that it expresses the buyer's deep feelings for his spouse in a way she is almost sure to appreciate.

Following a similar Consultation Protocol—**product knowledge, customer knowledge, F/A/B sales approach**—in any selling role will make you a consistently effective salesperson. Of course, it takes less time to follow the protocol than it does to read about it, once you have made it an automatic part of your routine. If you are in retail sales, especially, you'll be following your protocol as the customer walks in the door, so it must become second nature to you.

USE THE CONSULTATION PROTOCOL
IN COMMERCIAL SALES

You can use the Consultation Protocol in all sales arenas. But in those other than retail, you will have, and probably need, more time to develop the client information. Naturally, you will have found out the background information outlined above. But you will have to gather much of the information you need during the sales interview.

SET THE STAGE TO BRING FACTS TO LIGHT

Before you begin your probing, set the stage for the meeting. If you do this carefully, you can uncover facts and test your fundamental assumptions during the "preliminaries" so you can move more quickly to the "main event."

First, introduce yourself and who you represent, unless both are well known to the buyer. Second, briefly summarize what led to the meeting: "On the phone, you expressed a desire to hear about our new line of Japanese machine tools."

Next, state what you assume the client's overall goal to be, that is, replacing his company's existing machine tools. The client might reply that actually the company plans to expand its plant in the next year or two (a very vague statement calling for a follow-up question), and they will want to add new machine tools at that time.

BUILD ON THESE FACTS

Now, you already know your assumption is wrong and that you may be faced with a long-term selling effort. But you have also gained valuable intelligence: the company plans to expand. That probably means it remains fairly prosperous and wants to investigate the latest machine tool technology. That could mean a larger sale than you expected. (Or, it may mean the company is in trouble and is diversifying. Check this; you won't want to get involved in long negotiations for a big sale when hope of payment is remote. Of course, if you have worked up the background, you already know the prospect's financial condition, at least as publicly stated.)

At this point note, but do not belabor, likely benefits for the client: "Our machine tools may save you thousands in long-term maintenance costs, reduce the cost of retraining employees, and help you control labor costs."

During the early stages of your first sales call, ask how your client handles any pertinent aspects of his operation and how satisfied he or she is with the operation at this point. Of course, most clients will tell you basically how something works, but will be hesitant to admit that an operation or system is not functioning well. You will need to ask probing, follow-up questions based on your advance knowledge of the client's business and your own product line to determine those areas where you can really help and close a sale.

Use this exchange as a model for your probes:

• We've found, in tests of our own and competitive products, that many widget-winders tend to lose their strength when outside temperatures rise above 80 degrees. Has this been your experience?

The client might reply, "Well, actually, we've found that the Model 555 winder from XYZ Company tends to weaken at about 75 degrees."

Then you follow up with:

• Has that created a problem for you when you ship your boxes to Sunbelt states during the summertime?

The client might reply, "Yes, we've had a lot of insurance claims through various shippers, and the distributor in Phoenix occasionally complains about damaged goods."

Naturally, these exchanges are not likely to proceed at such a rapid clip. You will have time to exchange some small talk. During this time, use all your skills to probe your client further without his even knowing it.

UNDERSTAND YOUR CUSTOMER'S REASON FOR BUYING

Turning a client's state of mind in your favor, both in the short and long term, makes the difference between success and failure in consultative selling. It is not necessary to develop a complete psychological profile of each client: you are not a trained psychologist. But you do need information that relates to selling your particular product or service. You must understand your clients' business and personal goals, constraints, problems, and motivations *as they affect your line of business.* Then, you can recommend choices and promote your services that will fulfill these aspects of their requirements. Verbal probing, keen observation, and use of body language will go a long way toward creating this body of knowledge as quickly as possible.

Finally, once you've got a profile of who each particular client is, it will be helpful if you understand the reasons people buy. Sure, they need a new typewriter. Or their boss told them to replace the computer service company with one that would respond more quickly to emergency calls. But in addition to the factual reasons, people buy for a host of psychological reasons. And the psychological reasons may make the crucial difference between whether they sign a purchase agreement with you, or with someone else.

If you . . .

- –Offer a good product or service at an appropriate price (your company determines this)
- –Provide a well-developed professional presentation (you and your company develop this)
- –Show a pleasing consultative sales persona of your own (which you must cultivate and groom)
- –Display understanding of and concern for their stated and implied needs (which you discover through the knowing-your-client techniques outlined above)
- –And react to the reasons all people buy (which you are about to learn),

. . . **You will have the highest possible chance of making a sale.**

WHY DO PEOPLE BUY?
LOOK TO THE BASIC NEEDS

Clients buy to fulfill emotional needs and desires as well as business requirements, so you must at least understand a client's motivations. You'll find it perhaps surprisingly easy to uncover those motivations with simple questions.

Traditionally, salespeople have depended on persuasion to get the sale. After all, although your client may want your product or service, there's a huge gulf between wanting something and acting on the desire. What fills the gulf? Need, and for years, the best salespeople have been acting on it.

It is helpful to understand the basic attitudes that move *any* client to agree to purchase. Much has been written about Abraham Maslow's "Hierarchy of Needs" in reference to motivating employees. It is unfortunate that little has been said about how this hierarchy of needs relates to clients and customers, because many of these same needs motivate clients to buy. Maslow identifies basic needs that human beings want fulfilled. Some of these are life-giving, that is, adequate food, clothing, and shelter. But others promote or enrich life, including: acceptance or a sense of belonging, esteem, and so forth. These, especially, are important in sales.

REINFORCE THE NEED TO BELONG

Maslow identified that the need to belong is very strong in human beings, and giving them a group identity of which they are proud is helpful in any industrial setting. Likewise, your client wants to belong. You can recognize this, and help him want to belong to that special, very intelligent group of people known as "Your Clients" or the select group of people who use your products.

Study television and consumer advertising to see how important a sense of belonging is in selling to most people. Beer commercials, especially those shown during football games, invariably show groups of people or teams exerting effort and receiving positive results—catching the big pass, topping off a skyscraper, finishing a hard day's work—and celebrating the result with cold, sparkling beer. Many corporations encourage team behavior, and their buyers will most likely be very concerned about how their purchase fits into the team effort.

They may act very concerned that they be perceived as "scoring a touchdown" if they buy your product or implement your system. It is your job to prove to them that they *will* "score" and receive positive feedback and an increased sense of belonging to the group. By receiving positive feedback from you and their company, buyers also increase their self-esteem.

CREATE A TRUE SENSE OF SECURITY

Directly influenced by the sense of belonging is a feeling of security. The client will want to feel that he has chosen reliably, so that he will not feel out on a limb. He does not want to fail, so his sense of security ("I could lose my job if I blow this one!") may be threatened. He may not expect you or your product to be perfect, but he may insist on having enough assurance that it will perform adequately, and that you and your company will support your claims and your products' performance. You can help him feel that you will take care of any imperfections as soon as you become aware of them. Concretely, you can provide him a way to reach you when he needs or wants this sort of attention.

This sense of security is one reason new vendors or vendors of new products face such a hard time selling. Change creates insecurity unless a person has a reasonable assurance that change will not harm him or the source of his security—his job, his company, his family, himself, and his self-image.

This may form the important difference between market-driven and technology-driven sales. In the latter, only those few who feel secure and gain power and prestige by acting like pioneers or "early adopters," as the marketing phrase describes them, will buy new, "unproven" technologies. Market-driven companies, such as IBM, sell only those products for which the bulk of the market clamors. This is a much easier way to sell.

MAKE EACH CUSTOMER "STAR FOR THE DAY"

No one likes to feel like just another face in a crowd. Everyone wants to feel like *numero uno*. Although your client may want to feel part of the elite group that subscribes to your services or purchases your products, he will want to feel, at least when you're with him, that he is the primary subscriber or purchaser.

A sense of importance and a sense of belonging can cause conflicts, but salespeople with finesse reinforce the buyer's importance within the buyer's *own* area of responsibility and his sense of belonging to the larger corporate entity. You may imply that by buying your product, the client is the best, most important person in the department, *and* will gain the respect of the entire organization.

BUILD A SENSE OF PRESTIGE

Once you've found out, through probing, what will make your client feel all the other positive things, you'll need to emphasize those aspects of your product or service that will give him or her—and not anyone else—the feeling that signing on with you will enhance his or her prestige. For one client, the knowledge that your service is purchased by leading universities may provide that prestige; for another, it might be the simple fact that it is the highest priced in the field, or the lowest priced (if your service/product competes on price, and you position smart buying and low price as a package). In short, just because your last client was impressed and pleased by the fact that your delivery was by air express, don't think the same will please this one. Maybe you should soft-peddle that, when your probing shows you that prestige for this person means having access to your toll-free number, or something else you offer.

BECOME BIRDS OF A FEATHER

The fundamental approach to fulfilling these basic human "needs" requires understanding of the other person. When you understand another person, you recognize and accurately interpret that person's feelings, thinking, and behavior. You are not required to agree with, act subservient to, or act like, the client. It means that you recognize a shared membership in humanity, but appreciate the client's uniqueness at the same time.

In fact, you will find that people buy from *you*, and not from someone else because they feel you understand them better than your competitors do. Clients may need your products or services to fulfill business objectives, but they can probably find the same, similar, or even better ones from your competitors, or even do without and do quite well. Every top salesperson knows that people buy from people they like, and people tend to like other people who treat them as individuals. And to treat a person like an individual means that you share with them your recognition of their individuality.

In short, treat your clients as important individuals with feelings and experiences of their own. How do you translate this principle into practice? By seeking common ground with each client. This is called *empathy*. With empathy, you mentally place yourself into the world of the other person.

DEVELOP EMPATHY

Empathy means understanding the forces, pressures, and motivating factors that affect each client. This is why you need to know so much about your clients and their companies before making the first sales call. You are seeking to find conditions in which you can empathize with the buyer on both professional and personal levels.

For example, suppose you know the client's company had a tough year, with layoffs, budget cuts, tightened controls, and several shakeups at the executive level. You have an appointment to see the purchasing director, one step down from this executive turmoil. Ask yourself how you would feel in the same situation. You might think: "Well, I'd probably be in quite a bind. I may have had to lay off some staff and my budget might have been cut, so I could not buy everything other departments were asking for. I probably had to strain relationships, built up over the years, with other salespeople because I had to stop buying from them or had to cut back my orders, and I'd probably be darn nervous about what my new boss expected of me, and even more nervous about whether the next boss would approve of the decision I was making to please this one, however temporary it turns out to be. I would feel anxious and defensive, and I would be very hard to please, and very concerned about price and performance."

Even if you are wrong on some points, you will still feel a tinge of the purchaser's actual nervousness. You can make the call with at least a direction to follow in your sales presentation: emphasizing understanding of the director's dilemma (probably unspoken, since he may assume you are not privy to this information) and how you can help him achieve the best result at the least cost—both in dollars and personal risk.

On a personal level, you need to probe to find out what the client's interests and concerns are. If you both have children of similar ages, you can understand his concerns as a parent. If you both like dogs, you can share anecdotes about your pets' escapades. In short, when you find and seize the chance to make others feel and look good, you will succeed as a salesperson.

GIVE RECOGNITION IN ABUNDANCE

In addition to wanting to feel as if they are understood, people often desire recognition. Create opportunities for people to gain positive recognition for buying from you, and you can quickly establish the groundwork for a long-term relationship.

People who sound as if they want fame often want recognition. Your client might imply that "if this purchase works out, since its the first one we've bought, I'll probably be the talk of the company for my foresight."

Congratulate his foresight, but make your response as concrete as you can. Answer: "Not only that, but I'll be sure to send information about your innovative use of our product to our own company newsletter; we often have short articles on especially creative customers." And after the notice appears, you make sure a copy is sent not only to the client, but to the client's superiors if he requests it. In fact, offer to do it.

In any discussion with a buyer's superior, give the buyer all the credit for the positive results; *you* shoulder the responsibility for any problems brought to your attention.

Key parts of recognition, too, are thank-you notes, holiday gifts, invitations to interesting seminars or conferences, transmittal of interesting information or pertinent articles, congratulatory notes for personal, company, or family milestones (for example, you see in the local paper your client's daughter was named valedictorian of the graduating class at Jefferson High School), and many more. Misery may or may not love company, but joy, happiness, and celebration definitely revel in being shared with others.

SHOW RESPECT

As Maslow shows, people want prestige. Although you may not be able to grant prestige to your clients when they want it, you can give them respect. Your client says, "I'll be the only junior executive with one of these machines on my desk." You say, "That's great, isn't it? It shows me you're really on your way to the top, and all because you're a bit smarter than the rest."

You also need to convey respect for the person as an individual at every opportunity. Act courteously toward all of your clients. Show them with your polite manners and your willingness to listen that you respect them as individuals. Act attentively and sensitively toward them, their feelings, and their desires, and you will gain the intimate client knowledge you require to succeed. In short, to the degree you give others what they need, they'll give you what you need.

Okay. Agreed. But how can you find out what others need? Can you ask straight out? Probably not, unless you want to risk the relationship because of a hurried attitude. Blunt inquiries, especially early in the sales relationship, will understandably put the client off. Have you ever tried to buy a suit or a dress, and the salesperson said, "Well, what size are you, anyway? And do you want red or blue?" If that did happen, you'd feel insulted and leave. And rightly. You would have been treated as a commodity yourself—and one inferior to the commodity being sold. You wouldn't stand for it.

Can you ask others about the needs of the client? We've all had the experience, at one time or another, of someone asking questions about us—why we are leaving a job, whether we finished a report, why a client asked for a different representative—without asking us first or at all. It's not only insulting, but upsetting. No client will like that much.

Instead, learn to ask your client directly, but politely and completely, through a technique known as "probing." Just as you develop probing questions for your clients' product and service needs, formulate some that will give you insight into his position on the hierarchy of needs.

After you've practiced these techniques for the first time—and any other time you want to check up on your own consultative progress, as well as your client knowledge—work through the short checklist given in Figure 3–1.

Figure 3–1

SHORT EMPATHY CHECKLIST

Use this quick list of questions to improve your ability to empathize with each client. It is best as a handy checklist you can call to mind for each selling situation.

Before the Meeting

Ask yourself these questions about your client's possible motives and personality:

1. What do I already know about my client?
2. What does my client know about me?
3. What impression would this client have gained of me during our telephone conversations?
4. What possible business experience has my client had?

---

5. What prejudices and stereotypes may I have toward my client, and my client have toward me?
6. How knowledgeable is my client about my products and services?
7. What common ground do we share in our business interests? In our personal lives?
8. What does my client want or need from me and my company?
9. How can I best fulfill those needs?

During the Call

Keep these questions in the back of your mind as pointers to direct the flow of your presentation and your questions:

1. How is my client reacting to my comments?
2. What body signals is my client presenting? Negative, hostile, and skeptical, or positive, cooperative, and trusting?
3. Has my client shown any special interest in any points I have made or things I have said?
4. What points met with a negative reception?
5. What objections has my client raised more than once? Have I adequately responded to his or her concern?
6. How would I feel if my client was saying to me what I am saying to him?

After the Call

Take a few minutes to analyze each sales call and use the answers to build a foundation on which to base future sales calls.

1. What points were most convincing or important to this client?
2. Which points were least important, or most negative?
3. How can I relate what this client said to what others may say?
4. Have I learned any general lessons about people?
5. What did my client say needs to be improved, either in me or in my presentation?

BENEFIT FROM MODERN SALES TOOLS

Consultative selling requires you to keep in closer touch with more customers and know more about each customer than any other type of selling. You must also know more about your own product line and those of complementary or competitive products. Obviously, knowing so much about so many things requires a lot of time, energy, and brainpower—especially if you try to keep all of it in your head, on notecards, or written on sheets of paper.

Since the mid-1970s, modern technology has provided a range of sophisticated sales tools most salespeople either know little about or are afraid to use. Personal computers, voice store-and-forward systems, beepers and paging systems, mobile phones, electronic mail systems, videotape recorders, and even the humble answering machine all provide solutions to each salesperson's own greatest problem: making better use of limited amounts of time.

But, you object, "I don't have time to learn how to use personal computers. My clients hate answering machines. Beepers and pagers are only used by doctors and technicians." If you raise similar objections to these new sales tools, use your own techniques to answer your objections, overcome your own sales resistance, and sell yourself on their benefits.

Here are a few possibilities for starters.

ENGAGE IN CLOSE ENCOUNTERS

Keep in close contact with your customers. You obviously cannot physically call on them as often as you would like. Follow Joe Girard's example, and use word processors and a mailing list to send your customers monthly notes, even if it is just a greeting, your best wishes, and an invitation to call on you if they need any assistance. Before the age of computers, Girard did this and sent "Happy Occasion" cards to 13,000 customers each month.

He had a staff to do this, but you and your sales assistants can follow his example with a personal computer, a simple mailing list program, and a printer. In effect, you create your own direct marketing campaign.

REACH OUT AND TOUCH MORE CLIENTS

Second, you need to be more accessible to your customers. If you drive around a lot, you can make effective use of several modern tools: mobile or cellular telephones for your automobile, and beepers or pagers, especially the most current models that print out the telephone number of the person trying to reach you. With these, your customers can reach you when they need to. You can significantly reduce the time wasted and frustration caused by "telephone tag." You can also save money by reducing the number of long distance or repeat calls you must make. Customers will appreciate your accessibility, and realize appreciatively that you go out of your way to save them time.

DON'T LEAVE YOURSELF OUT

Third, continually sharpen your selling skills and keep up-to-date on how to present or demonstrate new products. Use a videotape recorder to practice various selling scenarios especially when changing or improving techniques, or presenting unfamiliar new products. Even if your company does not provide this equipment, you may already own a VCR and blank tapes, and you can rent a video camera for a few dollars a day. However, many companies will provide this equipment, and may already encourage the taping of training sessions.

Practice with this equipment as often as you can. Doing it only once or twice will not give you enough time to overcome stage fright. Get comfortable before the camera so you can deliver a reasonably relaxed presentation. Then, review the tapes and be tough on your performance. Practice until your performance matches your expectations.

Videotaping practice sessions is an absolute "must" for committee selling. Members of the selling team must practice their presentations, and other people from within your company should play the roles of your customers. They should be encouraged to raise objections and act as much as possible like the people you expect to see on the client's buying team.

Closely evaluate each team member's performance and discuss areas in need of strengthening. Then, repeat the session at least two or three times, refining your role and your presentation each time.

HELP YOUR COMPANY HELP YOU

Fourth, keep in close touch with your company, your sales support staff, your field service and customer support staff, and your fellow salespeople. How quickly your company reacts to a new sales lead, an incipient problem, a customer's simmering dissatisfaction, determines how long you keep customers' business. Electronic mail systems, voice store-and-forward systems, conference calls, and even teleconferencing and picture phones help you react efficiently to customers' needs and your company's communication requirements.

More sophisticated systems such as electronic mail and voice store-and-forward systems usually need to be implemented by the company itself. You could learn the basics of these systems and recommend that your sales executives study their potential applications and benefits to your organization.

If your company does not yet have these systems installed, you can approximate their sophistication with an advanced answering machine, call forwarding, conference calling, and similar telephone functions. You can retrieve messages from any phone anywhere with an advanced answering machine. The telephone company will forward any call to your number or to any other number with its inexpensive call forwarding service. You can also set up three- or multiple-way conference calls, allowing you to connect a customer with a customer service representative or service technician.

LET CLIENT MANAGEMENT SOFTWARE SHARE THE LOAD

Fifth, and perhaps most important, you need to keep better track of your clients and improve your analysis of which clients buy what products for what reasons at which times. A new type of computer software called Client Management Software allows you to achieve these objectives. Client management programs are available for every size sales organization from a one-person sales office to an international sales force.

Regardless of your company's involvement with automated client management and sales tracking, you can create your own relatively inexpensive, yet very effective client management system with a personal computer and easy-to-use programs. These programs range in cost from $49 to $595, and operate on commonly available PCs, usually the IBM PC family. For less than $2,000, you can purchase a complete system of computer, printer, and software, and you can almost certainly deduct the cost from your taxes as well (but ask your tax advisor to be sure).

Following are a few of the usually onerous tasks you can carry out with a client management program. You can:

- Store complete files on each client.
- Gather and store information on prospects.
- Analyze a large group of prospects by a number of characteristics or variables to determine who might make the most likely customers.
- Update client records quickly and easily, far more so than doing updates by hand.
- Generate sales letters from an automated mailing list of prospects.
- Remind yourself to follow up leads, make repeat calls, and call on current clients.
- Keep sales expense account records.
- Learn new sales techniques with training modules.
- Analyze successful sales techniques and show which techniques have been most effective with which clients.
- Identify possible cross-selling opportunities for other products or services your company offers.

As you can see, client management software may help you save time and effort where you most need it: in the niggling administrative details that make the difference between spending time to satisfy a customer and wasting time selling products a client does not want or need.

You may protest that you need help in the field, not in the back office. You may be mistaken. Time studies of salespeople show they spend between 60 and 70 percent of their time traveling or in their offices doing administrative tasks. It may well be worth your while to investigate these modern sales tools. One thing is certain: relatively few salespeople outside of the high technology fields use these tools now. You could easily gain a badly needed competitive edge.

EFFECTIVE CLIENT MANAGEMENT PROGRAMS

Here are brief descriptions of some client management programs for personal computers.

• **Sales Manager.**® Stores and analyzes information on customers and prospects; generates sales letters and mailing labels; identifies sales opportunities. Costs $575 and runs on IBM PCs or compatible machines. Published by Market Power, Inc., in Rough and Ready, CA (the real name of the town).

• **Sell!Sell!Sell!**® An extensive program for training salespeople, and usually sold to sales management for training new recruits. But it can be used to review basic selling and assess your own strengths and weaknesses in sales techniques. A second program, **Sell!Sell!Sell! Applications**®, lets you keep expense reports, manage prospect and customer lists, and keep track of when you need to make sales calls. It also identifies and analyzes which techniques work most effectively on various types of clients. This function is very extensive and produces an "objectives–features–benefits" chart to show how your products match a customer's needs and requirements. You can use the chart in your presentation and refine it as you learn more specific information. It runs on IBM PCs and compatibles. Published by Thoughtware, Inc., Coconut Grove, FL, the training module costs $495; the applications module, $295.

• **Saleseye.**® An inexpensive package, it keeps track of prospects, lets you analyze information about them, and identifies cross-selling opportunities. It also includes in most versions a simple word processor for sales letters, memos, and notes. It runs on IBM and compatible PCs, the Wang PC, and the Hewlett-Packard HP 150. Published by High Caliber Systems in New York City, it costs just $89.

• **The Sales Edge.**® The "grandparent" of sales programs, it remains one of the most sophisticated. Using programming techniques called "expert systems," it helps you interpret and understand your customer's personality. The program is divided into two parts: a self-assessment and a customer assessment. With the former, you identify your own selling strengths and weaknesses. It asks you a series of questions and you answer yes or no depending on whether you agree with the statements.

In the customer assessment, you are given a series of adjectives, such as talkative, aloof, hostile, egotistical, and asked to say whether you feel the adjectives accurately describe one of your clients. Then, the program analyzes your answers from the self-assessment and the customer assessment and lists various selling techniques and personal approaches you might use when you give a sales presentation.

Many large companies swear by Sales Edge® as a training tool, but you could use it to gain insight into how to deal with particularly difficult clients. It is published by Human Edge Corp., Palo Alto, CA, and costs $495.

These are just a few of the available client management programs and modern sales aids. Before you shy away from them, remember two things: first, these products were often invented by companies which were themselves looking for better ways to sell; and second, if you do not take advantage of these tools, your competition eventually will. Like adapting to any new tool, from hammers to computers, you will be a little nervous at first, and you will need practice. When you become proficient, you will make significant gains in productivity and increase the impact of your most valuable assets—your time and your brainpower. And you will more easily achieve an often sought for, but often missed, objective: excellent, accurate, and meaningful knowledge about each of your clients.

Chapter 4

THREE KEY QUESTIONING TECHNIQUES

A Workbook of Ideas

Many people think of salespeople as manipulators or seducers of reluctant customers; indeed, some salespeople think of themselves this way. It's easy enough to fall into that trap; you're getting lots of reinforcement from the many customers who respond to you as if you are trying to take advantage of them, or bamboozle them, or worse. And heaven forbid if they bought your product and were dissatisfied; they may have become outraged, even personally abusive.

People react this way because they believe deeply that they have been conned, and they usually feel conned because they feel as if they have been treated as an object, as a commodity, as just another face in the crowd. If the past, turbulent "Me" decade has taught any lesson at all, that lesson is this: everyone wants to be treated like a *person*. Someone who buys from you is not really a customer, a prospect, a client (although the connotation of "client" sounds better than the others), but an individual, a person. Even the toughest, most experienced purchasing agent in the hardest-nosed industry wants to be treated humanely, recognized as having personal problems and joys, situations and circumstances that require *your* personal attention.

DISCARDING TRADITIONAL SELLING CONCEPTS

TREAT THE CUSTOMER AS AN INDIVIDUAL

The heartbeat of selling consultatively pulses this message: Treat every client as an individual. The lifeblood of selling consultatively is identifying what the other person wants and helping make sure he receives it. The *brain* of selling consultatively is knowing this fact about human psychology: people hate to be *sold*, but they love to *buy*. This simple principle, pioneered by the Wilson Learning Corporation, is counter to everything most salespeople are taught. Most salespeople concentrate on getting what *they*, not what their customers, want. And little in the sales tradition encourages people to buy. That encouragement has always been considered a *marketing* function, somehow—ridiculously—separate from selling.

The traditional reasoning goes like this: Salespeople want first and foremost to make money. To do that, they have to make sales. To make sales, they have to convince prospects to buy. To convince prospects to buy, salespeople have to manipulate them into a buying mood. That's certainly making an uphill trek of it. The fact is, most people like to buy, if:

- They know or can be shown that they want or need the product or service.
- They perceive they are getting good value for their expenditure.
- They are treated well during the selling process.
- They receive the feelings they desire by buying your products or using your services.

Traditional sales fell into the trap because of one simple fact: buyers generally do not come right out and tell you just what they want and why they want it. You have to consult with them to find out. Or, of course, you could con them. But then you still wouldn't know what they wanted—just what you wanted to sell. And that's snake oil.

In many, if not most, selling situations, people will *not* tell you exactly what they want or need. Second, they may not know what they need. Third, they may *think* they know what they want, but they may be wrong.

ASK, DON'T TELL

How do you find out what people want or need, if they do not or cannot tell you? Of course, you *ask* them so you can help them buy what they want. Asking people questions to help you and them identify what they seek is called *probing*. You can ask questions in many ways and from many points of view. In consultative selling, *how* you ask a question means more than *what* you ask.

In the field of psychotherapy, researchers have learned through decades of trial-and-error in trying to *cure* their patients that the patients actually had to cure themselves. Psychotherapists found they could do no more than help their patients find their own cures. They had tried the well-known *directive* approach. A traditional salesperson would know this approach well: he tells his customers what he, the salesperson, *wants* them to buy.

Yet in psychotherapy, researchers, led by Carl Rogers, Karen Horney, Albert Ellis, and others, found that this approach had numerous weaknesses, and not surprisingly, these shortcomings are similar to those of traditional selling:

- These methods do not uncover the real nature of the problem, only what the psychotherapist (salesperson) thinks is the problem.

- Patients (clients) do not understand what they need.

- They are not willing to admit their problems to their therapist (salesperson).

- Patients (clients) must take action; psychotherapists (salespeople) cannot do it for them.

In short, the adage holds true: you can lead a horse to water, but you cannot make it drink. Patients in psychotherapy (and clients looking to buy) must both decide what they want, how they want to obtain it, how much effort they want to devote to it (how much they want to pay for it), and when and how they will be satisfied with the results of these actions. Psychotherapy patients and clients are not strange bedfellows; both are looking for solutions to problems.

SOLVE PROBLEMS: AID "THE URGE TO BUY"

In psychotherapy, this approach of helping people discover their needs and find solutions to their problems is called *nondirective* psychotherapy. It assumes that every person has a basic urge to live well and act in a healthy manner. Consultative selling likewise assumes people have a basic urge to buy because almost everyone has an urge to fulfill their basic needs and their not-so-basic desires. In modern society, for certain, fulfilling those basic needs and strong desires requires that people conduct economic transactions. In short, they buy, and generally, they enjoy buying.

As a consultative salesperson, a key part of your role is to help people enjoy the buying process, first through knowing what they want to buy, and second, by finding what they want or need to reach fulfillment.

ASK THREE TYPES OF QUESTIONS

The fundamental tool you need as a guide, a facilitator, a consultant, and a counselor is the ability to ask questions. Your questions, if they are pertinent and thoughtful, can lead your client along the path of discovery and fulfillment.

You can ask excellent questions as long as you remember this: All questions seek to know: WHO, WHAT, WHEN, WHY, HOW, or WHERE. As long as you know how to use those six simple words, you can formulate excellent questions with the three major probing tools, which are:

1. **General questions or fact-finders.** These are easy, factual probes that reveal objective information that you can verify. Here are examples:

   —*How* many employees does the company have?

   —*What* are its annual sales revenues?

   —*Who* is in charge of the tool-and-die plant?

   —*Where* is this plant located?

2. **Open-ended questions.** Open-ended questions elicit a wide range of information regarding companies, your clients, clients' feelings and emotions, their needs, and so forth. These questions cannot be answered with yes or no and usually begin with who, what, where, when, and how. They do not lead a client in any specific direction. Generally as you ask your first fact-finding question, you begin with a broad probe such as, "Tell me about your business," or "How do the marketing department's goals relate to the overall company's goals?" As your fact-finding proceeds, the questions become narrower, for instance, "What do you do in terms of training?"

3. **Closed-ended questions.** Closed-ended questions, which are not as probing as the other two, seek specific "Yes/ No" answers. Use such yes-or-no questions carefully, because they can end a discussion or interview with a client before you have determined his needs. However, closed-ended questions can be used to change the direction of the interview or discussion. For example, an effective closed-ended question could be: "Are daily trial balances important to your accounting procedures?" The question, "How important are they?" would, on the other hand, be a fact-finding, open-ended question.

   Other examples of closed-ended questions are:

   —Do you buy all your cleaning supplies at a central source?

   —Is there room in your budget for a new Broom Platoon?

(Warning: What if you get a "No" answer to the last question? You might as well pack it in and leave right then. So do be very careful of closed-ended questions. In fact, ask them only when you absolutely know what the answer will be, and you know it will be the answer you want. Then, a closed-ended question will help the client himself close a deal for you. "Is there room in your budget for a new Broom Platoon?" Answer: "Yes, several." If you get an answer like that, the client has just helped you sell him not only one, but several Broom Platoons.)

Each type of probe or question should *clarify, lead,* or *develop* clients' needs. To put to use what you read in Chapter 3, questions allow you to understand and empathize with a client, his problems, and the kinds of solutions he wants. Remember, too, that people buy from you because they believe you understand them, not because they understand or trust the product. They buy because they make a leap of faith, extending trust to you and your company.

All three types of questions—fact-finding, open- or closed-ended—can be used for one of three important functions; to clarify, lead, or develop. Each of these helps you and your client discover needs and solutions in these different ways:

- *Clarifying probes* may be used to:

    –Restate a client's comments.

    –Allow a client to respond to some point you have made.

    –Clear up a misunderstanding.

    –Encourage a client to expand on an idea.

    –Reveal what a client is thinking about.

    –Fill in gaps in your background/client knowledge.

    –Develop a shared base of information between you and your client about him and his situation.

- *Developing probes* may be used to:

    –Seek more information or more detailed information about a specific subject.

–Encourage a client to elaborate on a topic.

–Allow a client to express his feelings.

–Reveal a client's attitudes and beliefs.

–Help a salesperson elicit an emotional reaction from the client.

• *Leading probes* may be used to:

–Guide a client so he can gain a better understanding of his own needs.

–Enable you to move toward closing the sale.

To use a leading probe, you must first have used both the other kinds to determine whether the client wants to be led where you are planning to lead.

WORKBOOK PROBING SITUATIONS

It does little good, however, to consider these techniques in the abstract. Use the rest of this chapter as a workbook to learn how to use these probing techniques in various typical sales situations.

SALES SITUATION NO. 1

This is an actual example of a salesperson selling a package of public relations services to a growing high-tech company. Before the first interview, the salesperson had only a vague idea of what the high-tech firm wanted to accomplish, although the president appeared to want to use an internal newsletter to communicate with clients. Or so the salesperson thought.

First, if the salesperson had not already found the answers to these questions in her background research (knowing her client), she would have asked fact-finders, or general questions such as the following.

General Questions

• What is the basic nature of your current clientele?

The client explained that the company's business was to provide decision support systems, based on microcomputer technology, to corporations.

• Do you want to change that? If you do, how? What sort of clientele would be your ideal?

The client said that no, the mission of his company would remain the same. One of his objectives was to make better use of in-house resources and, if possible, use them to better serve clients and thus make more sales. The saleswoman here judiciously used a closed-ended question; it was not related to making a sale of her product, but it did let her know precisely where her client was or was not headed.

What other short and to the point fact-finding questions could you ask a similar client? Work up your own list; remember, to serve your clients you'll have to know who your clients are.

Clarifying Probes

Next, although the salesperson now understood the company's basic focus, the client's stated need for public relations services remained vague. So she asked clarifying questions:

• Do you see your main objective as creating a new profit center by selling a newsletter to your existing clients?

This question seeks to reveal a more precise direction in the client's thinking. If the client says yes, then the salesperson will know to pursue a tack that emphasizes a profit-making publication that will be sold like a regular newsletter. If the client says no, but does not elaborate, the salesperson will have to ask a second clarifying question. Two possibilities arise:

• Do you want to give it away to current clients? Or do you plan to use it as a marketing tool to gain new clients?

Think of additional clarifying probes based on the possible answers to this second round of clarifying probes.

In fact, during the whole question-and-answer process, the client expressed little knowledge about how to publish a newsletter. But he stated that his main goal was to increase sales of his computer systems at the lowest reasonable cost. So the saleswoman asked:

- In what ways do you now communicate with your current customers, and how do you reach potential customers?

This is an open-ended, clarifying probe designed to elicit a detailed explanation of the high-tech client's current public relations and advertising campaign.

Developing Probes

After receiving this explanation, the gist of the reply to the second clarifying probe was that the company had a satisfactory relationship with its advertising firm for print and radio ads and brochures. The sales department communicated with customers through brochures, personal sales calls, product/system demonstrations, and pilot programs. But the president emphasized that the company did not have a regular means with which to communicate to its customers important news about product enhancements, new applications, and most importantly, new add-on products and software that could be applied to their existing systems. In short, its customers did not often hear about the high-tech company in between sales calls. And the president felt his company's name was not being brought to the forefront of his clients' minds often enough.

With these details of the president's need becoming clearer, the salesperson needed to more thoroughly develop the details of the president's real need. Here is how she proceeded:

- You have also said that part of the mission of this company is educating its clients and prospective clients. What forms have you thought that education would take?

The president responded that he wasn't sure, but he knew more advertising would not educate his customers, and he didn't want to hire more salespeople so each could spend more time educating fewer customers. Either way he knew wasted his resources. But he knew other companies used newsletters, and he knew he already had an internal newsletter filled with excellent information. He also thought it would be a good idea to try to make some money from it.

Now it became clear to the salesperson that the president wanted to use his existing technical newsletter as the basis for a tool with which to communicate more effectively with his own current and prospective clients. His desire to have a profit-making publication was clearly less important than his need to communicate more effectively with his clients.

However, the PR saleswoman needed more information about the high-tech firm's shortcomings in educating and communicating with clients. So she asked:

• What specifically has prevented you from fulfilling your client education mission so far?

The president replied that his salespeople often failed to read the internal newsletter and even more often failed to suggest to clients the new applications or new uses for their systems that his technical researchers had developed and published in the internal publication. His salespeople just did not have the time to backtrack.

Now, the saleswoman began to see the light. The president wanted to use his existing newsletter for several purposes: (1) to keep his company's name in the forefront of his clients' minds, (2) to provide up-to-date, accurate information about new applications and new products his clients might need, and (3) to provide an inexpensive way to help his clients sell *themselves* on buying more of his company's products and services. With these needs and goals in mind, the salesperson began to ask leading questions to bring the president toward a decision to purchase services she was *about* to offer.

Are there other questions you can think of that would have helped the saleswoman clarify the situation more clearly or more quickly?

Leading Probes

With all her facts now established, the saleswoman was ready to help her prospect think about the solution she wanted to offer, one she had determined that her company could provide and that would also fulfill her prospect's needs.

"From what you've said," she told him, "I can see that you either have to learn to live with incomplete service, as you define it, or add staff or contract labor to carry it out. Is that so?"

The president said yes, he knew he would have to spend some resources, but he did not want to add new staff. He figured if he was going to do it at all, then he would need outside help.

• What do you see as the advantages of adding contract labor with a public relations company to do it?

After asking this question, the saleswoman added a brief commentary: "I agree with you that, as you believe, there is no one on your staff with the public relations and newsletter production experience you need to provide the professionalism your public image demands. As I see it, you want a professionally prepared product on a regular basis, but prepared with the excellent information your staff develops. Is that right?"

She already knew the answer would be yes; she simply led him to express it, so that they could both act upon it.

After these and similar probing questions were asked during two hour-long meetings, the salesperson presented a package of newsletter editing services based on the high-tech firm's internal technical publication. It included:

1. Editing of the lengthy technical newsletter into a lively and concise sixteen-page, semimonthly client newsletter filled with "briefs" about new applications for existing products and

potential applications for new products and systems. It would be free to current customers for six months, and a $50 per year subscription would be charged thereafter to help cover production costs; it would be given free as a premium or incentive to new customers for six months as well.

2. A two-page monthly "New Product Alert" broadside, giving a brief description of "hot" new products and seeking direct responses from customers concerning their interest in these products. Each envelope would contain a prepaid postcard on which a customer could circle a number and then drop it in the mail. The postcards would go directly to the high-tech firm's sales department for immediate follow-up.

3. Mail list management services, handling the printing and distribution of up to 1,000 newsletters per issue, starting with 250 copies and building to 1,000 copies by the end of one year.

The president of the high-tech firm agreed to the package of services and the salesperson signed a one-year agreement for a reasonable and profitable monthly fee. And the high-tech firm agreed to cover printing and production costs and expenses for mailing and distribution.

Selling public relations and advertising services has long been a bastion of consultative selling, but the difference here was this: although the PR firm indeed had experience in editing newsletters, it had never done so for a private client before. If the public relations salesperson had kept to traditional selling, she would have told the president, "Sorry, I can't help you with a newsletter, but I can offer you twenty-five excellent ways to get your firm's name in the trade journals." But the president of the firm was already doing a good job of getting his name in *The Wall Street Journal, his* clients' "trade journal," and that was not what he needed. Instead, the salesperson asked probing questions, and used her firm's available expertise and resources (or expertise it could easily hire) to develop a package of services the high-tech firm *needed.* Naturally, she had already gotten agreement from the principals in her firm that the newsletter she proposed to sell was a direction her own company wanted to pursue.

In sum, she participated with the client firm's president, worked through a process in which she helped him clarify his real need, and developed a package of services to fulfill that need. *She discovered a need and fulfilled it, both for her own company and for a new client.* She produced a classic win-win-win situation.

SALES SITUATION NO. 2

You also need to ask questions to remove a prospect's "preoccupation barricade." Not every client, perhaps not even very many, have your sales presentation as their top priority. How often have you arrived at a call to find a client nervous, upset, harried, or preoccupied by something else that was happening in his or her life? How often have you been welcomed with open arms as if your visit was the high point of your client's day? Compare the two, and you will see that when you arrive to make a sales call, you must first break through a client's preoccupation barricade. Asking questions, giving clients a chance to participate in the discussion, showing them that you really care about their answers allows you to make constructive use of breakthrough techniques.

Consider a situation in which a salesperson sells financial and banking services to corporations and local businesses. She calls on treasurers, comptrollers and chief financial officers to offer them a range of some 200 available financial services. Suppose her main product at the moment consists of cash management services. She knows a bit about the prospect company, its product line, and its reputation, but she knows very little about its current cash management practices.

She will need to use all her questioning techniques. First, she will need to ask fact-finders, also called by some experts "bridge" questions, that allow her to discover facts she needs to present the proper services and move from the social pleasantries to the business end of the sales call.

Fact-Finding Questions

She may need to ask several fact-finding questions, such as:

- How do you currently collect your receivables and re-mittances?
- How do you provide money for your payables and dis-bursement accounts?
- Do you earn interest on your overnight deposits? This is a closed-ended question that will lead to a fact-finding question.

If the answer is yes, then she would ask what current rate of interest is earned, on what basis the interest is paid, and so forth, seeking to find points on which her services offer a competitive advantage.

If the answer is no, she could ask a clarifying question:

- How much cash do you keep on deposit? From there, she would ask a leading question: Did you know you could earn X dollars per month in interest income with interest-bearing overnight deposits?
- Is your current cash management procedure satisfactory? But this may be too closed-ended; a better question might be: How does your current cash management procedure stack up against your expectations? Without saying, "Have you got problems with . . ." this question allows raising a problem without impolite bluntness.

What other fact-finders could this financial services salesperson ask a commercial customer?

Clarifying Probes

Once you begin to solicit facts, and plug gaps in your knowledge, you expand your knowledge by asking for clarification. In the financial services example, this may include exchanges such as these:

- You say you now earn 7 percent interest on your deposits. How is that compounded? Daily, weekly, monthly?

- Is the interest paid on the daily balance or on the *average* daily balance for the month? (She could also explain what the difference between the two is if the client appears confused.)
- How often does your current financial institution post your interest income in your statement?
- What and how much does the institution charge for checks and deposits?
- Do you require us to return cancelled checks with your statement?

Suppose the treasurer answers that he suspects he earns about 7.25 percent interest, and he believes it is paid on the average daily balance. The interest income is included in the monthly statement. The company pays 25 cents for each check and 50 cents for each deposit, and so far, the company had required all checks to be returned by the bank.

Think of two additional clarifying questions you could ask the businessman.

Developing Probes

From the information obtained above, the saleswoman can see that she needs to add more depth to her understanding of the client's need. In fact, so far he seems pretty satisfied with his current bank, so why is he seeing her? She needs to ask satisfaction questions which measure the client's emotional reaction to his current institution. In short, she must use developing questions to find out how he feels. Using such questions will show you more of what you need to know, and, more importantly, may help a client clarify and recognize his own feelings and problems by explaining his views to you. In short, he may identify, clarify, and intensify to *himself* his own feelings. That is what you want to accomplish; the better a client understands himself, the more easily he can express that understanding to you—and the more easily you can fulfill his needs and make the sale.

Here are some sample questions that the saleswoman might have used:

- Most treasurers say they object to paying more for deposits than checks. How do you feel about charges for checks and deposits?
- I recently read that company treasurers are being asked to make more interest income to boost company profits. How do you feel about your role in making your firm profitable?
- Many of my clients say they are disappointed with the service they receive from their cash management services. How do you feel about the service you receive from your current bank?
- According to the *ABA Journal,* some banks are pushing their clients toward electronic funds transfers among corporations. How do you feel about the trend toward these transfers among corporations?

She has discovered with a developing line of questions that the treasurer appears to be faced with intense pressure to increase interest earnings and reduce banking costs. She is now moving toward the treasurer's "hot spot," and needs to ask leading questions.

Developing questions can be used, too, to ask specific questions about any competitive offers you know the client may be considering actively.

Leading Probes

Now, you can ask questions in such a way that the client responds favorably to those services and products you have to offer. Here's an example of what the saleswoman might have done:

- It appears you need to increase your interest income on your cash deposits. Would it be just as satisfactory if you also *saved* money on the cost of your cash management services?

Here, you could explain to your client that your institution charges less for checks and deposits and show how those savings could equal an additional half a percent of interest income over a year's time.

• Would an interest rate that increases with the amount on deposit—each day—help you? For example, if you have on deposit $50,000 for one day, that day you will earn 7.5 percent, not 7.25 percent.

And so forth. Continue asking leading questions to determine whether your services match his needs, and how your services can be flexed to fit his needs.

What other leading questions could you have asked this corporate treasurer?

SALES SITUATION NO. 3

In this situation, *you* work through an actual list of questions you have recently asked a client. Use each of the types of questions discussed, and jot down the client's answers and your follow-up questions. Then, write down what could have been improved, and formulate more consultative questions and responses.

My Sales Situation

Remember, you ask questions first to help a client identify his or her own needs, and second to help you identify how your products and services can fulfill those needs.

FACT-FINDING QUESTIONS AND RESPONSES

1.

2.

3.

4.

How Could I Have Improved These Questions?

1.

2.

3.

4.

CLARIFYING QUESTIONS AND RESPONSES

1.

2.

3.

4.

Additional Questions I Could Have Asked

1.

2.

3.

4.

DEVELOPING QUESTIONS AND RESPONSES

1.

2.

3.

4

Additional Developing Questions

1.

2.

3

4

LEADING QUESTIONS AND RESPONSES

1.

2.

3.

4.

Additional Leading Questions

1.

2.

3.

4.

HOW TO ASK:
A SHORT COURSE IN QUESTIONING

Here are more tried and true ways to ask questions. Use them to uncover facts, clarify situations, reveal a client's feelings, and lead a client to your solution to his problem. Think of them as tools to help you improve your own questioning process. With each method, several examples from different lines of business are given.

FACT-FINDING QUESTIONS

- **How many:** Ask "how-many" questions to quantify a client's business operations or family situation.

  –How many children (pets, relatives, visitors, guests) do you have?

  –How many trucks are in your fleet, how many need cleaning (repairs, lubricating, oil changes, etc.) every day?

  –How many plants (factories, offices, field offices, facilities, mills, etc.) do you have?

  –How many products (mistakes, service calls, etc.) do you make in a day (week, month, year, hour, quarter)?

  "How many" questions are, of course, cousins to "how much," "how large," and similar questions.

- **What kind:** Ask "what-kind" questions to learn specific details.

  –What kind of car (truck, computer, machine tool, evening dress, makeup, cookies) do you have (own, use, lease, rent, wear, eat, operate, like, prefer, etc.) now?

  –What model (size, shape, color) of widget (tire, car, cabinet, bathroom fixtures, house, abrasives, etc.) do you have now?

- **Do you:** Ask "do-you" questions to learn how a client now accomplishes a goal or carries out a necessary process, or to learn more specific details about a client's needs.

–Do you now use (drive, buy, have in mind, do your own, etc.) your car (computer, calculator, recreation room, garage, den, family room, etc.) for business purposes?

–Do you have in mind (want, prefer, like) a particular type (model, style, size, shape, color, etc.)

- **Is it too:** Ask "is-it-too" questions to clarify your understanding of the client's situation or need.

  –Is your current car too small (large, old, expensive to operate, etc.)?

  –Is your office space too crowded (underutilized, too far from downtown, too expensive, too close to downtown, etc.)?

- **Are you thinking of:** This type of question can begin the transition from a fact-finding or clarifying question to developmental or feeling-revealing questions.

  –Are you thinking of changing your method (process, means, mind, etc.)?

  –Are you thinking of sending your children (pets, parents, employees) to private school (obedience training, on a vacation, to a conference, etc.)?

DEVELOPING QUESTIONS

- **How do you feel:** This type of question straightforwardly asks a client to express her emotional reactions to a situation.

  –How do you feel about sending your children (employees, salespeople, etc.) to summer camp (to off-site training courses, on cold calls, etc.)?

  –How do you feel about prospects for improved business conditions in your (oil refining, automobile sales, T-shirt, cruise ship travel) business?

- **What is your opinion of:** This question does not use the word "feelings" which some clients may react to negatively. But many people will express an opinion and subconsciously show their underlying feelings and beliefs when the word opinion is substituted.

  –What is your opinion of the job your current service (representative, financial institution, etc.) is doing for you at this time?

  Related to this question are questions that begin with:

  –How satisfied are you with . . .

  –What do you think about . . .

  –What is your attitude toward . . .

  –How happy are you with . . . and so forth.

- **Does this mean anything:** This type of question avoids the traps of asking for feelings or opinions and may more specifically reveal a client's true need.

  –Does the fact that the new tax law stretches out the depreciation period for investment real estate make any difference to your goals?

  –Does the development of a new 2,500 horsepower compressor mean you can speed up your process?

  Similar questions would include phrases such as:

  –In what way does this affect . . .

  –Are you concerned about . . .

  –Does this worry you . . .

  –Is this important to you . . .

CONVERSATIONAL GAMBITS

You may need to use conversational gambits to precede feeling-revealing questions to deflect any negative reactions to your probing questions. Some people instinctively try to hide their feelings, and you need to keep their reactions from being aimed at you, especially in potentially emotional situations, such as selling insurance, selling someone's home, selling funeral services, selling medical care services and medical insurance, selling educational services, and the like.

Learn these techniques and gambits well; they are similar to those you can use later in answering objections or presenting a "testimonial" close. Tell an anecdote or pithy story, cite a specific example, list several needs or problems that similar customers have cited, or use a generalized lead-in that reflects the thinking, feelings, opinions, or attitudes of other people. For example:

- I recently called on Jim Jones, buyer at ABC Foods, and he told me that he had used our new shrimp peeler and felt it had saved his people about 15 percent of their effort. Do you feel your shrimp peelers give you enough productivity?

- John Smith at Pity Packaging says he feels the trend toward plastic containers will mean increased savings for food manufacturers and more convenience for consumers. What do you think about this trend?

- My other packaging clients tell me they face three main problems: (1) the high cost of paper packaging, (2) the large amount of storage space paper boxes take up, and (3) how easily paper tears or gives way. Do you find you face similar difficulties?

- Most of my customers tell me . . .

- Many surveys I have read show . . .

LEADING QUESTIONS

- **Do you agree that:** This question elicits a positive or negative answer, and enables you to gauge your progress in finding out what customers need and whether they are ready to buy.

  –Do you agree that your company needs to save 20 percent (reduce costs by, increase your profit margin by, etc.) of its fuel costs (with increased productivity, with lower labor costs, etc.)?

–Would you agree that the color blue better accents your pastel furniture?

- **Does this seem:** Similarly, this question evokes a response that indicates customers' agreement or disagreement with the direction in which you have been leading the discussion.

    –Does this proposal (offer, discount, profit margin, etc.) seem reasonable to you?

    –How acceptable does this model (size, shape, color, quantity, delivery date, etc.) seem to you?

- **How helpful:** This and similar questions also nudge a client toward a close.

    –How helpful would it be if we could make these widgets in black and red, the color scheme you seem to prefer?

    –How important is it for your widgets to be in black and red with blue stripes?

Use these questions as springboards to improve the quality of your own questioning techniques. Even more important than how you formulate your questions, however, is how you ask them (politely and thoughtfully). More important still is whether or not you hear your clients' answers—not only what they *say,* but what they *mean.*

In the next chapter, you'll be reintroduced to what is perhaps the single most important ingredient in a successful consultative selling formula—**listening**.

Chapter 5

LISTEN TO YOUR CLIENTS

The Secret of Consultative Selling

All the probing in the world, and all the knowledge of what makes buyers tick, won't help you understand them any better if you do not do one simple thing: **LISTEN**. Don't let the term "consultative" throw you. In many ways, you are like a doctor, consulted for your expertise. And it is true that no doctor in the world could make an appropriate diagnosis and prescribe the correct treatment and medication if he or she failed to adequately hear and understand what the patient said.

True, a doctor probes her patient's anatomy, discovers the patient's vital signs, runs tests, and so on to make a diagnosis and prescribe treatment. But what makes the patient feel reassured or confident in his recovery? Not the probing, prodding, and sticking; all of that makes him feel uncomfortable. A patient gains confidence when he knows the doctor is really listening to what he has to say.

Clients are no different. You can probe and prod and give advice, but you will not make a sale or begin to build a relationship until you listen.

A lot has been said about listening since Sperry Corporation made it the focus of a national advertising and public relations campaign several years ago. Yet, it remains one of the least understood functions of a salesperson's job. What is the purpose of your job? No, not to make the sale; rather, your real job is to help a client find solutions to those of his needs and problems which you can affect with your products and services.

In consultative selling, asking questions allows your client and you to identify his true needs and problems. Even if your client clearly identifies his problems to you, you cannot recognize them if you are not listening. Only with intense listening can you understand and then suggest and promote the correct solutions. You can accurately answer objections only if you heard what the real objection was in the first place. You can quickly close a sale only if you hear the client tell you she has already made a decision to buy. Remember that true selling works when you help your clients to buy, not manipulate them into being sold.

For example, suppose a client has resisted your entreaties and presentations for weeks or months, throwing up objection after objection. And you met every objection when it was made with a considered reply, yet the client still would not buy. What would you think? Probably that the client was a pain in the neck, had no intention of buying from you, and, in fact, enjoyed wasting your time.

LISTEN TO THE <u>WHOLE</u> STORY

On the other hand, suppose you had let the client ramble on, had ignored his early objections, and let him express the whole problem? Consider this actual example from a real estate sale. The couple had looked at a house they liked, but they complained to the agent about dozens of minor problems and potential hassles: cutting down trees, resodding the lawns, patching the roof, so forth and so on. Instead of offering reassurance, the agent let them talk, asking some seemingly mild, but interested questions. In the middle of the discourse, the agent asked, "You seem to know a lot about real estate. Have you ever owned a home before?"

The couple said, "No, we owned a small investment

property once, and boy, did we take a beating on that. It was a disaster."

Bingo! Skyrockets went off in the agent's head. She thought, "They want to buy this house. They like it a lot, but they're afraid of making a mistake. They feel they may assume the same problems the investment property obviously gave them. It's my job to reassure them that owning their own home—without the hassles of tenants and their wear and tear—will be much different. And, I'd better work to make buying this house as trouble-free as possible." She did just that. She provided the needed reassurance, calmed the buyers down, and made the sale. And as importantly, she followed through and made the closing process as smooth as she could. In fact, sensing that her clients wanted to avoid being the pushers, she took on the problems of prodding the mortgage lender so that the sale would be closed on their timetable.

However, if she had spent her time telling the couple the roof didn't leak, the resodding would not be expensive or necessary, the trees would provide shade in the summer, and so forth, she would have exasperated the couple with her constant interruptions. Instead, she listened and listened and waited for the heart of the matter to be revealed. In fact, she never had to answer those specific objections at all.

In short, listen to *everything* a client has to say. You never know when the diamond will be mined from the coal.

USE THE PERSUASIVE POWER OF LISTENING

You've already learned that clients have to sell themselves. They must make the leap from doubt to belief, from inertia to motivation. Traditional selling states that the salesperson's job is to shove clients along the path to a decision. Do that and clients will invariably *know* they have been shoved and, sooner or later, resent it.

Consultative selling holds instead that you can lead clients along the path, but you have to let them find their own direction. They have to talk themselves into buying. And they cannot do that if you ask too many questions. You have to let them talk and you have to actively listen. What does listening accomplish? Much. Consider these points:

- Clients get the chance to state their ideas about their needs and problems.

- When people talk, their feelings and reasoning become clearer to themselves as well as to you.

- Clients often sell themselves by revealing their real problems to themselves. In the example above, the couple had buried their irrational apprehensions under a rational "cloud" of making the best buy. By talking about their previous mistake, they confronted their fears, recognized the possibility (but not probability) of failure, and decided to go forward.

- Listening allows clients to think more creatively. The expression, "Two heads are better than one," may be re-evaluated in this light; two heads are better than one if one listens to the other. By feeling free to express themselves, clients often reveal deeply buried ideas and concepts.

To summarize: listening helps a client make important discoveries for himself. You must give a client the chance to fully participate in the process of finding solutions to his own needs and problems.

Consider what often happens in domestic quarrels: a spouse only grudgingly agrees to do something the other spouse wants to do. The thing turns out badly to the embarrassment and expense of both. The reluctant spouse may then retort, "Well, it wasn't my idea in the first place."

Similarly, if you "sell" a client without his honest agreement and that sale goes wrong, you will undoubtedly hear: "Well, I didn't want to buy it in the first place. You sold it to me. Take it back and I want a full refund." This reaction means the person feels he was trapped into buying something he didn't want, and you *personally* broke faith with him.

However, if a client persuades himself by talking the problem through and making his own decisions based on your participation in finding solutions, you will probably avoid a negative reaction.

THE "ACID TEST" OF
CREATIVE, EFFECTIVE LISTENING

As you learn any other selling or personal interaction skill, you can learn to listen more creatively and effectively. By following these steps, you can pass the ACID TEST of creative listening. The ACID TEST is an acronym for actions you take to help yourself hear and understand what a client is saying. These are outlined below.

You need not use all of these actions to make yourself listen during every sales call. Learn them all and use them as tools in a kit to be wielded when you need them.

A FOR ANALYZE

As a client speaks, you can analyze what she says. In the back of your mind, ask yourself: "What does she mean?" "Is her statement an opinion, a wish, or a fact?" "What information do I now have to confirm or refute her statement?" And so forth. A also stands for Attention: giving someone your mental attention and paying attention to what she says.

C FOR CONCENTRATE

To really listen, you must concentrate on the actual voice, the words as they are spoken. To concentrate, you need to make frequent eye contact. Look at your client and become involved in what she is saying and *how*—that is, the body language she uses to say it. You cannot really hear what someone is saying if you look at the ceiling, out of the window, or at your watch. So focus your mental processes by your physical actions. In the same way, you can begin to control a client's thoughts by adjusting her body posture and gestures, first, of course, disciplining your own body language and its responses to your client.

I FOR INTERPRET

As you learned in Chapter 3, people often do not say what they mean. Thus, to listen and understand, you need to interpret to yourself—and to your client—what she has actually said. You can use probing questions to verify or refute your mental interpretations of a client's statements.

For example, suppose a client says, "I don't like this color green." How would you interpret this statement? The client does not like the color green, or she does not like the particular shade of green you showed her? A correct interpretation would be that the client did not like *this* particular shade of green, but was not adverse to the principle of the color green and probably would not mind being shown a different shade. You could follow up with a probe such as, "If you don't like this shade, what shade of green do you prefer?" That would elicit two key results: (1) It would determine whether or not she really disliked the idea of the color green, and (2) It would encourage her to participate in making a choice and bring her closer to a buying decision.

D FOR DELIBERATE

When a client pauses, or goes back over already covered ground, you can deliberate on what she has said to this point. This helps you isolate and remember her key points and enables you to use a powerful sales tool. That tool is the ability to repeat key sentences to your client after you have heard her out. Saying something like, "Mrs. Smith, you said a while back that you were not interested in blue begonias . . ." provides positive proof that you were *listening*. Since most people really do not listen to anyone else, they do not expect you to do it either. When you *prove* that you were listening, you often make a powerful impression that stays with a client.

T FOR THEORIZE

As you analyze and deliberate, you can also project or develop theories about what someone really means and what they may say next. Ask yourself *why* a client has made the points she has made, particularly those points she has made forcefully or repeatedly, or some points you feel she should have made, but skipped over. For example, suppose a client never mentions price. You could think she believes price is no object, but you know from experience that your price for this product is higher than any competitor's. Does that mean she doesn't know the competition, or does it mean she has no intention of buying. Perhaps she is on a "fishing expedition" for more information. In short, theorize and read between the lines.

E FOR EXERCISE

As a client speaks, you cannot sit passively. Passive hearing quickly leads to distraction, and you will find that you haven't heard a word, much less listened to what your client meant. Listening takes mental and physical *exercise*. Lean forward in your chair. Rest your hand on your chin, and look at your client. Perk up your ears, that is, actually "aim" your ears toward your client. Put your feet flat on the floor. Even if you find your client less than scintillating, acting "as if" in this way will help get you where you want to go.

S FOR STUDY

Whereas deliberation implies a slight mental withdrawal from your client, study implies a mental movement toward your client. In science lab in high school or college, you studied a specimen under a microscope by looking intensely and thinking actively about what you saw. In the same way, listen to your client by looking intensely and thinking actively about what she says and how she says it.

T FOR TUNING IN

Just as you tune in to the right channel on a radio to hear your favorite music, so you must tune in to the client's "wavelength" to understand what she actually means. You cannot hear and understand if you tune out a client's voice and tune in the noise of your own thoughts, street noise, voices from a hallway, or any other sounds. More importantly, tune in so you can recognize the client's relevant points and help her explain those points more fully. In the real estate example above, if the agent had tuned the young couple out, she could have heard the statement about the previous real estate investment, but responded, "Oh, isn't it nice that you already know so much about buying a house." That statement would have meant the agent was really thinking, "Oh good, now I don't have to waste my time teaching these beginners what a contract and a mortgage are. Boy, that will save me a lot of time." Of course, she would have missed the single relevant statement the couple had or would make.

You can tune in most effectively when you actively extend a feeling of empathy toward your client. You really listen when you desire to share her feelings, needs, and problems. You each feel more like a person, and you make your client feel as if she is being treated as a valuable and special individual.

The ACID TEST of listening can serve as a multiple choice quiz in which you find the right answers—how to best serve your clients—every time you make a sales call.

BREAK BAD CONVERSATIONAL HABITS

As much as you need to identify your clients' real meaning, you'll want to avoid bad habits that will turn your clients off. As people speak, they look at you and respond to your reactions to them. If you look bored and disinterested toward someone who is enthusiastically exclaiming about what a wonderful product your company has, undoubtedly by the end of the sales call, the client will doubt not only your belief in your product, but her own. Learn to avoid these bad habits; listening to your clients won't do you any good if what they hear when they "listen" to you is a turn-off.

DON'T INTERRUPT THE SPEAKER

Detailed research has shown that interrupting someone plays a part in a struggle for authority or dominance in a conversation. In consultative selling, you do not want to wield authoritarian power over your clients; you want to share with them and encourage them to participate in the decision-making process. Thus, it is important that you not interrupt clients, even when they say something outrageous, provocative, or wildly inaccurate.

It is hard for salesmen to restrain themselves, especially when selling to a woman. Abundant research shows that men interrupt women nine or ten times more than women interrupt men. And women have a much harder time reasserting themselves after they have been interrupted. You will lose a woman's attention by seeking to dominate her by dominating the conversation. It appears that women learn to smile sweetly and accept the interruptions or verbal dominance. But they very wisely react by rejecting the man who does it. If you are a consultative salesman, that means you lose the sale. In traditional sales, you may have badgered a woman into buying, a tactic perfected by some door-to-door salesmen, but it is inappropriate in a consultative situation.

Saleswomen, on the other hand, have the opposite problem of listening too passively and never getting a word in edgewise, especially when selling to male clients. However, at least in consultative selling, listening too much often works better than interrupting too often.

NEVER CONTRADICT YOUR CLIENT

Just as rude as abruptly interrupting a client is contradicting him. Failure to contradict does not always signal agreement. In fact, contradicting means you are acting aggressively and hostilely to a client. Instead, make judicious use of the "yes, but" technique to rebut or correct what a client has said. You can use the same technique to move a client from a negative direction or train of thought to a positive one.

For example, a client says, "I don't know if I need to buy this today." You wouldn't say, "Of course you need to buy this today." That's contradicting the client. More appropriate would be to say:

"I understand your apprehension, but wouldn't you like to take advantage of our 10-percent-off sale today?" or "We only have a limited supply. If you think you'd like one later, I can hold it for you with a small deposit." Layaway plans are a time-honored and successful tool to induce clients to buy today products they really don't need until later—and, more often than not, to lead a wavering client eventually to a "yes" response.

AVOID GETTING TOO CASUAL TOO FAST

Many sales manuals advocate calling clients by their first names as soon as possible after you meet. You are instructed to probe for their names quickly and then call them by their first names or a diminutive form of that name. In consultative selling situations, however, that can be deadly. First, it assumes a friendliness and familiarity which encroaches on the person's privacy. Second, it assumes an equality of status that you may not have achieved. And third, it creates awkward situations when salesmen are selling to women and when saleswomen are selling to men. Then too, especially if you use a nickname or diminutive without being invited, it can create instant negative feelings.

For example, my business partner's name is Robert, and he strongly prefers to be called Robert. He says that 90 percent of the time when he speaks with salesmen, they immediately and without asking permission call him "Bob." He almost always contradicts them at once, and says, with an edge to his voice, "Call me Robert, please." And that's only the half of it. He would really prefer to be called Dr. Bach.

Saleswomen face a different problem in addressing their male clients. If they call male clients, "Mr. So and So," they risk being treated as an inferior. If they call men by their first names, they risk having their behavior interpreted as a social or sexual advance. It seems preferable for saleswomen to call male clients, especially older male clients, by "Mr." And in an introduction, calling him "Mr." should be accompanied by a firm, businesslike handshake which a saleswoman offers to the man. Combined with conservative, but "chic" business dress and a businesslike attitude, saleswomen can overcome either of the misinterpretations. But—and this is a Hobson's choice—dealing with the inferior position, if one is assumed, may be easier in the long run then dealing with the problems that assumed familiarity can lead to.

If salesmen call women clients by their first names, it assumes both a personal familiarity and a superiority or male dominance. Salesmen would do better to ask women clients what they prefer to be called to avoid confusing and embarrassing situations. Some women want to be called "Ms."; others prefer "Mrs." or "Miss"; others will invite you to call them by their first names. Of course, a salesman should *never* call a woman client by possessive, derogatory terms, such as "dear," "honey," "darling," or any other chauvinistic term.

By asking a woman's preference, a consultative salesman shows politeness and respect to a woman client in a society sadly lacking the simple courtesies. It will enhance a salesman's image as being a cut above the rest.

Here's how salesmen can handle the situation of being introduced to female clients.

1. Introduce yourself: "Hello, I am John Smith, sales representative of XYZ Wax Company."

2. Politely ask her name if you don't know it: "And please, what is your name?" Or, "I haven't had the pleasure of being introduced to you before. You are?" You may already know the woman's name, or in many cases, the woman client will remind you before you have to ask.

3. The woman may reply, "I'm Mrs. John Jones," or "I'm Mrs. Gladys Jones," or "I'm Gladys Jones," or "I'm Ms. Jones," or "My name is Gladys."

If a woman introduces herself by her title, "I'm Ms. Jones," or "I'm Dr. Jones," and does not quickly add, "But call me Gladys, please," you can safely assume she wants formality preserved. Do so. She may later ask you to call her by her first name; she may not. Of course, this process works very similarly with men in business situations, though it may be relaxed, for either gender, in social ones.

Calling people by their first names also signifies business status as well as socioeconomic and class differences. In most businesses, superiors have the leeway to call their subordinates by their first names. The same does not hold true for subordinates unless company policy *and* practice puts everyone on a first name basis, or a boss specifically tells an employee to call him or her by first name.

Of course, true equals in a company call each other by their first names, even diminutives and nicknames, from the start. So, if you call a person by his or her first name without permission, you assert your equality or even superiority. You cannot assume that status without a client's permission.

What you call someone also depends on their age and social position as well as on their socioeconomic or business status. For a young salesperson of either sex to call an older woman by her first name without being asked would be very presumptuous. Equally bad would be for a younger—and that is a relative term—salesperson to call an older businessman or prominent person by his first name.

In short, follow one of these steps before addressing someone by first name:

- Ask for permission to call a client by his or her first name, or
- Wait until you are invited to call someone by first name.

By the way, etiquette experts say the *only* acceptable response to an introduction to another person is the social question, "How do you do?" Knowing this will also help establish you as someone who is socially a cut above, almost always an asset in consultative selling.

PITCH YOUR VOICE FOR POWER

Numerous experts, including John Molloy and Nancy Henley, have shown that society interprets a person's knowledge, authority, and status by the pitch of the voice—deep or shallow, high or low. Men with high-pitched voices are viewed as feminine and weak and are ignored or made fun of. Women with high-pitched, girlish voices are seen as shrill and stupid. Neither gets any respect at all.

Consider the 1970s TV character Ted Baxter, the klutzy anchorman on "The Mary Tyler Moore Show." Audiences thought the way he dropped his voice to assert himself was very funny, but it shows the truth of common perceptions about voice pitch. Off the air, Ted Baxter spoke in a somewhat high-pitched and often whiny, wheedling voice, and even squeaked or squealed on occasion. The staff ridiculed him. But on camera, Ted Baxter's voice dropped, and although what he said most of the time was inaccurate or nonsensical, Baxter retained authority for his audience.

So, both men and women in sales should learn to deepen the pitch of their voices to enhance their image of knowledge and authority. You must be careful not to fool yourself about this. Consider these everyday situations and compensate for them during your sales calls:

1. A person's voice tends to rise and the pitch get higher when he or she is nervous or under stress. Since every sales

call may create stress, remember that your "normal" speaking voice during a sales call may be higher than when you are speaking to your friends or office mates.

If you are nervous speaking before an audience, you will really have to watch your pitch.

2. The longer you speak, the more your voice tends to rise. You strain your larynx as you speak, and the result is a higher pitch, especially if you speak without interruption for more than fifteen minutes or so. Modulate your voice and listen to your tone. If your throat begins to feel tired or uncomfortable during a long presentation, you can bet your voice is rising, causing a lowering of the positive impression you were making on your audience.

3. Telephone transmission of your voice tends to raise its pitch, so you may need to drop your pitch a little when speaking on the phone to present a consistently positive image.

4. Excited or agitated people tend to speak in higher-pitched voices, so remember to temper your enthusiasm for your product so you do not jeopardize your knowledgeable image.

Voice pitch is especially important to women. In broadcasting, experience shows that women with lower pitch who work in broadcasting tend to be hired more often than women with higher pitch. Weigh your own sales experience. By and large, who are the successful saleswomen? The ones with soft, high feminine voices, or those with deep, slightly less than but close to, masculine voices? Since broadcasting and sales both depend on creating impressions of knowledge and authority, experience proves that women with lower-pitched voices do better in sales.

CONVERSATIONAL TRAPS
SALESWOMEN CAN AVOID

Similar to the differences in voice pitch, women tend to phrase their sentences differently than men do. As a result, they get what they want less often than men. Women tend to ask indefinite questions that eschew responsibility. For example, a question such as, "You really prefer the gray suit, don't you?" avoids making a direct statement or demanding a straight answer. Women tend to use this form of question very often. Men tend to ask direct questions ("Is this the place?") and make direct statements ("This is the place"), the latter even when men have some doubt about their own correctness.

Furthermore, women tend to make more requests for what they want and men tend to make more demands and issue commands for what they want. A woman who really wants to buy a yellow dress may say to a salesperson, "You think I look nice in this yellow one, don't you?" A man buying a new suit will state, "I want this gray one," although he might look over his shoulder at his spouse for confirmation. Men might gruffly say, "What do you think?" but they would be hard pressed to say "You think I look good in this gray suit, don't you?" Thus, saleswomen may need to put more definition, more forcefulness behind their sales pitches.

A DIFFERENT SCHOOL OF THOUGHT

On the other hand, there is a school of thought advocated by some successful saleswomen that saleswomen should capitalize on their feminine advantages. One very prominent commercial real estate broker in New York with a staff of twenty saleswomen urges them to send their male clients personal notes and flowers, take them to lunch, use flattery and compliments to stroke their male egos. Apparently, this approach makes their sales pitches irresistible.

In another example, a saleswoman had been trying to break a contract impasse with a male senior buyer for almost a year. Her male counterparts had not only been unable to break the logjam, but had made the situation worse. Severe clashes of male egos, like two rams butting heads, had occurred. So, she decided to defuse the situation, and invited the senior buyer to an expensive lunch. She dressed nicely, but not suggestively, and spent a great deal of the lunch listening to the buyer's tale of woe. The result was that the logjam was broken within the week, and the sale was completed.

However, this pull-out-the-stops approach can be dangerous. It could cause some men buyers to assume the compliments and niceties were come-ons or sexual invitations. If a man makes such an assumption, but is refused, it could easily lead not only to lost sales, but also to the spread of nasty rumors about your morals. Hell may have no fury like a woman scorned, but scorned men are not exactly known for heavenly behavior either.

EARS TO HEAR, WITH DISCRETION

You cannot hear every verbal message or grasp every non-verbal message a client presents as he talks to you. We all look and listen selectively. The key is to learn to *hear* those things that are truly meaningful to you. Train yourself to hear the messages that are relevant to your task. Your job, again, is to identify the client's problem, and that problem, simply put, is the difference between what a client has and what a client needs. So, your main listening objective is to identify those two and then clarify what is important to your client in fulfilling the need.

To accomplish this objective, you must respond to your clients whenever you identify their key concern or motivating factor. You want to encourage your clients to explain in more detail so that you can reinforce several things. You want to:

- Prove you are truly paying attention, which makes a client feel good about you.
- Reward your client for doing the "right thing." In your case, that means moving toward or adopting your solutions to his or her needs.

- Reinforce your client's feelings of self-worth and build self-confidence.

In most social activities—and selling is a very social activity—people want rewards. If you reward them or reinforce their positive behaviors, they tend to repeat the same or similar behavior to continue to receive the rewards. However, many sales experts overlook a person's tendency to want greater rewards for continued positive behaviors. They face other pressures and influences which tend to increase their demands for greater rewards. Consider your own desires to get paid more this year than you were paid last year. Why? Probably because prices are higher so you have to spend more to obtain the same goods and services, *and* you feel you need a bigger and better reward, not the same or a similar one.

With reinforcement techniques, you can reward a client's positive behavior, but be aware that you will need to modify and often increase the size and type of reward, even in the simplest conversations.

FIVE REINFORCEMENT TECHNIQUES TO USE

Here are five ways to reinforce and reward clients as you listen to them discuss and clarify their problems.

REWARD NO. 1: NONVERBAL OR BODY LANGUAGE REWARDS

These would include leaning forward toward the speaker, smiling with approval, and nodding the head positively. Many people feel insecure when they speak and need constant reinforcement. To avoid spending half a sales call agreeing with everything an insecure client says, use positive, nonverbal signals.

Results from dozens of experiments on the effect of rewards in normal conversation show that rewarding body signals produce very positive, even amazingly positive, results.

REWARD NO. 2: SPOKEN PRAISE

Any appropriate expressions of approval serve as spoken praise and you can use them during brief pauses between a client's statements. Phrases such as, "That's very interesting . . . I didn't know that . . . Oh yes, don't you know it! . . . Good . . . Really?! . . . You really have strong feelings about that . . ." and so forth. We use them every day in normal conversation. Recognize their effectiveness and test the change in your sales results as you begin to respond with combinations of spoken praise and positive body language.

REWARD NO. 3: "UH HUH"

Even a nonspecific mumble, such as "Uh huh," when said at the right moment, will reward people's behavior and encourage them to repeat that behavior. You need only say "Uh huh" or make a similar sound in a positive manner at those points you *want* to reward. All the evidence shows that you will quickly find your client's behavior will change in the direction you want it to.

REWARD NO. 4: PLAY BACK THE "TAPES"

When you want to reinforce a particular point, or shift a client away from a negative one, repeat or play back the desirable or positive statement, or put a positive light onto a negative statement and change the direction. For example, Mr. Smith has just finished saying he thinks your product is priced right, but the quality leaves a lot to be desired. To reinforce his opinion about price and change it about quality, you could say, "Mr. Smith, I'm glad you agree that we have the best prices, and I understand your concern about quality, but did you know that *Widget World News* rates our widgets among the top five widgets in the northeastern corner of Massachusetts?"

Repeating what someone says provides a very strong

reward. It appeals to a person's sense of self-worth. When you repeat something to the speaker, a person appears to tell him- or herself something like, "Oh, he agrees with me. Therefore, I must be right, and if I'm right, I want to stay that way, so I'll keep agreeing with him." Sooner or later, that becomes fixed as a "fact" in a client's mind.

REWARD NO. 5: APPROVE AND PURSUE

Combine these four rewards as you listen: approving nods, appropriate expressions of agreement, "uh-huh" at the right points, and paraphrasing, in your own terms, what the client says. Then, to encourage your client to keep talking—in the direction you want—ask the client to explain or expand on his thoughts, and reward him by implying that he knows more than you do. Use sentences that begin like: "I don't clearly understand . . . Can you show me what you mean . . . What do you mean when you say . . . Why does this mean so much to you . . ." and many more.

These five rewards form a very powerful and persuasive combination. An example will show you how effective: Larry Wilson, a noted sales trainer, who should know most of these tricks since he teaches them to thousands of salespeople each year, tells a story about how he was set up to be "reinforced." He says he planned to introduce the reward idea to a group of insurance agents, but warned the vice-president about what he was going to do. So, the vice-president told his agents to do this: when Wilson talks about rewards and walks to the right of the room, act very interested, really follow him with body language. But when Wilson moves to the left of the room, look the other way, ignore him.

Wilson recounts that it took about five minutes for him to start climbing the wall on the *left* side of the room. Of course, the vice-president and the group broke up laughing and told Wilson he had been "reinforced."

So, use rewards and reinforcement for several aims, including:

- To encourage a client to explain in more detail a positive point or opinion, a sticking point, a confusion, or anything that seems to bother him or her.
- To encourage a client to talk more about needs and problems that *your* products and services can solve.
- To discourage a client from straying from the main theme of the discussion.

In short, the more you listen and reinforce clients' comments, the more they will participate in the discussion. As they participate, they will reveal to you and to themselves the real nature of their problems and how you can help them solve these problems.

LISTEN WITH EMPATHY

You have been advised to use empathy to understand your clients' point of view. You uncover their point of view and feelings by doing background research and asking questions. You *share* their feelings by listening and extending your own feelings toward your clients. You best empathize by sharing what you yourself believe you heard your client say. Play back or feed back your understanding to your client and elicit his reaction to your understanding. You are not judging the other person's feelings or opinions. You don't say, "I believe your opinion is this and it's wrong." Instead, you would say things like, "So, my understanding is that because we shipped you three incomplete orders last year and that slowed your production by two weeks, you are wary of ordering from us again. I am unhappy also because I want to work with you, and our shortcomings prevent that. Let's see if we can improve our ordering and scheduling for your next delivery."

Other phrases you can use to preface your empathetic remarks include: "Let's see if I understand correctly what you are saying . . . So, you seem to believe . . . Do I understand what you are saying? . . . In other words, you maintain that . . ." and so forth, through numerous familiar phrases.

Say these messages with open, yet confident body postures and gestures, and in a calm, soothing tone of voice. You can't share with someone else if you send mixed or confused signals. And although you don't wear your heart on your sleeve or emote like an insincere movie star, you need to feel empathetic toward your client's position. If you don't feel it, don't fake it.

WALK AND TALK A FINE LINE

In traditional sales, salesmen were perceived as dominating, powerful figures—from the imperious, but gentlemanly Victorian purveyors, to the backslapping Willy Loman, to the snake-oily Professor Harold Hill. In consultative selling, salespeople must tread a fine line between being too overbearing (domineering, pushy, even bullying) and too passive (soft, yielding, retiring.)

This rule is especially true when a consultative salesperson speaks and interacts with a client. In many ways, consultative selling requires what used to be thought of as "feminine" qualities: understanding, accepting, reassuring, almost nurturing behavior. Yet, you must also express the so-called masculine qualities: knowing, producing, affecting, informing, acting-with-authority behavior. Notice, however, that the so-called masculine and feminine qualities are neither mutually exclusive nor contradictory. They are, in fact, complementary. Any salesperson can incorporate these qualities into his or her sales presentation. They will not make a salesman effeminate or less masculine, and could well make him more appealing to women buyers. Nor will they bestow upon a saleswoman unbecoming machismo; they could well make her appear more business-oriented to men buyers.

In short, "customize" your personal presentation to each buyer as much as you customize the package of products and services you recommend to solve a client's problems. It is likely that without a customized personal approach, you will not get the chance to customize your solutions.

In fact, *before* you present any solution, you must use these techniques to first and foremost reach an understanding with your client in two areas:

1. How the problems and needs are defined
2. The most likely reasons for those needs and the origins of those problems

With this agreement, you can move forward to develop and present solutions.

Chapter 6

GREASE THE HINGE

Overcome Objections With Positive Feedback

Call it The Motivator, call it a Hot Button. Call it what you like. It is still the single most important thing that makes your customer want to buy. I call it THE HINGE. Why? Because, like a door, your customer is ready to swing open or slam shut, depending on how you move him. And, like a door, your customer can be blown shut by the wind—that is to say, he is subject to direction by other forces, including his superiors' wishes, a change in his company's financial status, a sudden gust of assertiveness by one of your competitors, and so on. This is why, naturally, you've got to get a firm grip on the Sales Handle. You get this by finding out what each customer's Sales Hinge is— what he is interested in, both in business and possibly in private life, what he wants from this deal, and so on.

The purpose of much that you have learned before— knowing clients, asking questions, listening well—can be summed up in one phrase: Finding the Hinge.

Here is a summary of what you've accomplished up to now:

- You have identified and clarified the situation and the client's background.
- You have gauged the buyer's emotional reactions and feelings.
- By asking the appropriate kinds of questions, you have identified the client's stated needs.

- By interpreting body language and listening, you have derived his true concerns and needs.
- You have reviewed your understanding of those needs and problems and clarified any misunderstanding.

With these steps completed, you will have a good idea of what the client's Hinge is.

WHY YOU NEED TO FIND THE HINGE

Why do you need to know each client's Hinge? *First,* every step in consultative selling circles around it. You cannot close the circle and the sale without finding the Hinge and moving it with your Handle. *Second,* it helps you treat each client and his situation individually; it helps you avoid laundry-list recitations no one wants to hear. *Third,* it encourages you to act as a consultant to each customer in a professional, competent, active manner. *Fourth,* it enables you to fulfill your primary purpose: creating the feelings and results the customer wants.

HELPS SPARK THE URGE TO BUY

Most importantly, knowing the Hinge enables you to help create, or spark, a client's urge to buy. The goal of any substantive sales call should be to create a conflict in the client's mind—a conflict that results in the urge to buy. This mental conflict arises over what the client has now—his current situation—and what he wants or needs—a mutually beneficial and practicable solution to his problem or need.

The reason you ask questions, probe carefully, gain understanding, and all the rest is to help a customer identify those needs and problems; once he has done that, he will be in even greater conflict than before you helped him think about them. By using your client's Hinge correctly, you can help him swing toward the solution you propose. In effect, you are an *Illuminator,* shedding light where darkness reigns, or a

Facilitator, enabling the client to find his way, at last, through a wilderness.

You have listened patiently, ratified beliefs, and gently guided your client so that he may discover for himself what he wants. You've emphasized the emotional benefits and positive feelings your client will feel by relieving his inner conflict or by solving his overt problems. And you've prepared him to consider your product or service as the best, most definite, most readily available solution to his problem. But still, he may have some concerns, and you'll have to answer them to make a sale.

REQUIRES FLEXIBILITY AND SENSITIVITY

Throughout all of this, you have been alert. Now, as your client begins to express his concerns, you especially need to stay flexible, always listening for the tip-off that identifies the direction in which your client wants to go. You'll need to act sensitively in several ways.

First, stay sensitive to your client's physical and emotional reaction to you personally. Work to stay on positive, upbeat terms with each client, and don't even attempt to apply to one buyer tactics you would apply to another. For example, Mr. Ardry, sales manager for a specialty coatings company, had made many calls on the buyer for a food packaging firm. Both had enjoyed talking about football. But the buyer was ill during one call, and the purchasing VP received Mr. Ardry instead. Without thinking, Ardry launched into an enthusiastic, ten-minute monologue about Sunday's big game. He failed to notice that the VP's eyes first glazed over in boredom, and about five minutes into the monologue, flared in anger at the salesperson who was wasting his time.

Second, act sensitively toward the client's own situation. Most clients do have numerous outside pressures that may prevent them from buying what you want to sell. Act with empathy in these situations. For example, a manufacturer's rep who had done a steady business with a clothing buyer for eight years suddenly ran into stiff sales resistance. He knew that the buyer's company had just fought off a major takeover battle and was selling off numerous divisions to retire the enormous debts the battle had incurred. With some probing questions, the salesperson found that his client's purchasing budget had been slashed. Even worse, it appeared the client would not get his annual raise. Since the buyer had a young child and an expensive condo, he was worried about his family situation. The sales rep could have acted very disappointed and tried to make the buyer feel guilty that he did not buy his line anymore. That would have made the buyer feel worse, and no doubt, would have given him a motive to exact subtle revenge on the salesperson in the future, when his budget was back to normal. Instead, the salesperson sympathized with his client, acknowledging that he had heard how bad things were—that the client's company was, indeed, confused and disorganized, and so forth. He established a bond with the buyer, and elicited a commitment from his client to buy his products as soon as the crunch had eased.

Empathy and understanding did both of them a lot of good. It let the buyer off the hook, and it maintained an important relationship that had taken the salesperson years to establish and lots of effort to maintain. In such a case, this is the next best thing to a sale—since a sale could not occur in any case.

TREAT "OBJECTIONS" AS LEGITIMATE CONCERNS

Notice that in the previous case, as so often happens in selling, this salesperson could not overcome his client's objections. In fact, like many so-called objections, they were actually legitimate concerns over which the buyer had no control.

That phrase—*legitimate concerns*—seems far more appropriate to a consultative salesperson than the hackneyed word, *objections*. Using the latter term fosters the image of the adversary buyer-seller relationship that consultative selling seeks to avoid or replace. Although some buyers may use various ploys to put you off, behind these ploys lie serious concerns. Salespeople too often are taught to do two things:

- They are taught to attack the ploy without probing for the legitimate concern.
- They are taught that if they cannot get past or around this to the order, it is their fault.

Neither is a good idea. The first will result in nothing anyway; the second results in the same loss of sale, with a bundle of bad feelings for the salesperson—the last thing any of us needs.

Rather, sales professionals should understand that buyers may use put-offs because they feel they are defending themselves from selling tactics when they know, for one reason or another, that they cannot make a favorable response. They may say no when they mean a variety of things. Here are some possible reactions, followed by possible reasons to probe for:

- "Don't bug me. I'm very busy and preoccupied with something else." In this case, find out what the "something else" is about, and relate empathetically to it.

- "I don't need your product." Probe and find out what products or services the buyer has now and his level of satisfaction with all facets of them.

- "I'm tough and I'm going to make it hard on you." (This may be implied rather than stated.) Ask yourself why someone might want to do this. It could indicate personal immaturity and defensiveness, and you should react calmly and sensitively.

- "I'm not convinced yet." Ask more questions because you have not yet found the Hinge nor have you accurately identified how his need and your Handle coincide.

- "I need to be reassured so I can present this to my superiors." The buyer is nervous about making the right decision. Give him confidence in his impending decision to accept your solution and advice about how he can best present his decision to his executives.

• "I have a few questions I want answered." Review your understanding of the progress so far, and elicit any uncertainties the buyer has.

• "I am a professional buyer, and I am testing your competence, depth of knowledge and persistence." (Again, you will probably perceive this as an attitude rather than hear it as a statement.) If this appears to be the case, react professionally and persistently; faltering in the face of such a negative response would seriously damage your ability to make the sale.

ACCEPT OBJECTIONS AS NORMAL

If you follow the lessons of earlier chapters, you should less and less often encounter the flat "no" and the common put-offs that buyers often use to avoid traditional sales pitches. In traditional selling, too, salespeople are encouraged to immediately reply to, if not trounce, an "objection" as soon as the buyer raises it—as if it were some disgusting disease needing to be eradicated before it spreads. In traditional selling objections are seen as ways for clients to squeeze out from under the salesperson's thumb to avoid buying what he wants to sell.

In consultative selling, you do not pounce on objections. First, you might interrupt your client. Second, you will be giving the objections or concerns more importance than you want them to have; you realize they are legitimate questions to the buyer, no more no less, and not an impediment to a sale. So, as you learned earlier, you'll do best to repeat the concern, ratify it ("I understand your concern about the color, but let's get the size and style decided on first," you might say), and move on with your probing and presenting. Somewhere, later on, answer it fully.

Legitimate concerns form an essential part of the process by which you and your client clarify muddled thinking and perceptions, correct misperceptions and misinterpretations, relieve apprehensions and fear, identify needs and the means to fulfill them, and explore solutions to problems.

And as importantly, legitimate concerns may identify for

you obstacles and problems you cannot, at that moment, overcome.

In general, buyers do not agree to sales calls just to waste time. Of course, buyers sometimes want to gather information, compare your prices with your competitors', and so forth, but usually you have the chance to make a sale during every sales call you make. Therefore, consider any concern a legitimate one until something proves it otherwise.

Furthermore, if you have listened carefully, you can distinguish between a valid concern and a diversion designed to shift your attention in a different direction, often one in which you do not wish to go.

THE BIG WHY:
THE KEY TO CONSULTATIVE CLOSINGS

Any concern a client raises involves the Big Why. He is saying directly or implying, "Why should I change?" Unless a client has a very bad situation that must be handled immediately, each will be reluctant to change, even if he has asked for the sales call. Almost every concern is based on a "Why change?" question lurking in the background. Your task becomes presenting sound reasons for change and creating a solid foundation for it so your client feels reassured and confident about making the change.

Remember, most customer complaints and dissatisfactions arise from frustration and disappointment. Behind them lies one reaction: "You, you rotten salesperson! You convinced me to change when I was happy with what I had. Now, this new thing has failed, and I am worse off than I was before, and it is your fault!" By helping the client assume the decision to make the change—that is, to place the order—you are also avoiding possible recriminations if, for any reason, dissatisfaction results. (Naturally, you will also not promise anything you cannot deliver. And you will act as liaison between your company and your client whenever needed and whenever prudent as well.)

Although there are dozens of questions that ask "why change" and statements that imply it, typical ones pop up repeatedly. They are phrased somewhat differently in each industry, but the meaning remains the same. Knowing them and how to respond prepares you to meet the concern and move that much closer to closing a sale. Following is the single most common concern, and some appropriate responses.

"STICKER SHOCK" REVISITED

The most common concern in any industry is price, and price concerns have become almost second nature to any buyer. Early put-offs about price—"You're too expensive"— before you've even quoted one can easily be ignored. Just as often, toward the end of a sales interview, price put-offs can be closing signals. A buyer is ready to buy, but may need more definitive information, or reassurance that he is getting a good bargain for his money, or he may have some reservations about the price for the projected benefits. Here is a very common price objection and a good example of how it was handled in a tough but fair consultative manner.

• Why should I pay your price when I can get one just like it for less?

This can be a difficult one, especially if you know your price is higher than many competitors' prices. A sales manager for a semiconductor manufacturer faced a serious concern about this, but found successful and mutually beneficial answers. As you may know, selling semiconductors during the mid-1980s was a very price-competitive business with prices falling as much as 50 percent or more per year. Yet, vendors must have broad product lines, very high quality, excellent on-time delivery records, and competitive prices.

This sales manager faced a situation in which a previously solid customer had received an enormous order for computer components. Of course, this brought competing semiconductor salespeople out of the woodwork. The buyer was offered a very low price the manufacturer knew it could not match. In response to this unusually low bid—an obvious attempt to snare a new customer and grab market share by a company prepared to take a loss on the order—the seller asked the buyer straight out: "What are your price objectives? That is, what price do you need to be profitable?" The buyer came back with a price between the seller's previous price and the very low bid.

The seller responded by proving his company's strong support for the buyer, and he also established a condition of his own. The seller emphasized that his company had supported the manufacturer when it had just started out and *no one else* would even ship to them. He also reminded them that his firm had even bailed the manufacturer out of a tight spot when another vendor had missed a desperately needed shipment of semiconductors. He reiterated his firm's performance and strong and continuous support and noted that it might not be available from the low bidder.

The buyer acknowledged the support and performance, but wanted a better price than the price of the year before. The seller compromised on the price, but established its terms, including the condition that the contract be firm for twelve months. The seller wanted to avoid returning again and again to renegotiate the price every time some adventurous competitor needed a quick sale.

The outcome? An order for two million parts at a price guaranteed for twelve months, *and* a mutual recognition that if the buyer came back with a request for a lower price, it would mean the end of their relationship. That was something the buyer did not want to do. In fact, after the twelve-month deal was made, the buyer's purchasing agent called the seller and told him that his competitor had in fact come back with an even lower bid. Since it occurred during the agreement period, the buyer did not accept it—nor did he plan to for the coming year because he did not want to end a pleasant and mutually beneficial arrangement over a few dollars.

IF ALL ELSE FAILS, USE THE BIG PICTURE APPROACH

The most effective response to the "I can get a better price" concern is the Big Picture Approach. In this response, review the "big picture" about your company's products, service, features, benefits, performance, and so forth. Emphasize all your product's features and benefits, compare them favorably to your undercutting competitors', and show your client how much more value he will obtain by paying your slightly different price. Meet any price concern with solid reasons why your client will receive maximum value for the money he spends, and if accurate information is available, how and why your competitors may not match your big picture. In short, create a positive price/benefit ratio in the client's mind.

You can also ask "big picture" questions to uncover more specific details of a buyer's price concerns. For example, instead of responding directly to a price question, you can ask:

- When you say our price is too high, to which competing product (or service), exactly, are you comparing our price?
- To what are you comparing our price when you say you believe it is too high?
- You may have a point, but let's make sure we're comparing apples to apples. What products are you comparing to my company's?

If you have a solid knowledge of your competitors' products and their price structures, you should know in advance the strengths and weaknesses of your own product line as they compare to others. Then, if competing products do better on some features than yours do and vice versa, as they invariably do, you can shift the questioning to the Big Picture.

Instead of getting into a picky, niggling feature-by-feature competition, you may say:

- XYZ Corp. has some fine products, but I believe if you compare our service, support, maintenance fees, delivery schedules, terms, and our complete customer support package, you will agree that our firm better meets your needs.

- Let's compare our complete service to the one you cited. Could you explain first what our competitor told you about his company's offer?

This approach shifts the focus from a narrow comparison to a comparison of a broad base of products and services. In case you've missed it so far, emphasis on service, support, delivery schedules, quality, training, terms, and so forth are the hallmarks of the consultative approach. Commodity pricing and undercutting price competition usually have little place in a consultative approach. But the Big Picture can also serve tactical selling purposes. Here's how:

1. You can use it to help clients compare alternatives and more easily reveal to themselves their real needs.

2. You may find out details of competitive products and offers you had not known about.

3. You may discover steps a client may consider taking on his own, without your, or any other vendor's, participation.

4. You may uncover unfair or inaccurate comparisons stated by your competitor to your client.

What advantages does the Big Picture bring you? First, you honestly and accurately justify your higher price. Second, you show how some features and benefits may mean more to a client than others, justifying paying your price for them. Third, you explain the actual differences in *value* to your client. For example, a client may be concerned that your price is 10 percent higher than a competitor's. But he may be more concerned—and favorably—about your one-year warranty as compared to the competitor's ninety-day warranty, and your four-hour service response time compared to the competitor's twenty-four-hour response time.

In short, in consultative selling of any type, never discuss price without taking your Big Picture into account. It is too easy to fall into traps that could bring a sales call to a screeching halt, box you into a corner, or convince you to make price concessions before you need to do so.

In fact, the best attitude you can take toward price and similar concerns is to treat them as only one feature of your product and service line. Use the F/A/B (features-advantages-benefits) approach when you discuss price, and avoid getting upset or nervous when a customer mentions price. Believe in the quality of your offer and stress its benefits to your clients.

BEYOND STICKER SHOCK: OTHER LEGITIMATE CONCERNS

You can expect customers to express their nonprice legitimate concerns in many different ways. Given below are brief explanations of and responses to the most common ones:

"I DON'T NEED YOUR PRODUCT"

Related to the "Why should I buy now?" question, this concern may indicate that: (1) the buyer is telling the truth because he has an adequate inventory, or (2) the buyer is clouding a different concern, such as a budget freeze or lack of money. Probe to determine the real reason behind the put-off. If the client does not give a legitimate reason for the put-off, then respond with ways to reduce inventory or make better use of existing supplies, or describe any discounts or promotions, or discuss likely future price increases.

"I'M NOT INTERESTED"

If you have done your homework, you should know whether or not the client is likely to be interested. If you have been granted an interview, then the person is most definitely interested in something about your products. Probe for the specific areas of interest, and raise several reasons he should be interested in: increased productivity, higher sales, more profits, more efficient manufacturing techniques, greater personal prestige, more luxurious and satisfactory lifestyle—whatever it takes to find the Hinge.

"I'M SATISFIED WITH MY CURRENT SUPPLIER"

Too many salespeople accept at face value the, "I'm satisfied with my current whatever (supplier, sales rep, agent, vendor, etc.)" response to their solicitations. In selling their goods and services, agents often fail to probe into the specifics behind this statement. That's too bad, because *no one is ever entirely satisfied with anything.*

If a prospect says he is satisfied, *never* criticize or denigrate his current supplier. Your client feels a bond between that supplier and himself, and any criticism will be interpreted as an attack on the client. And you will almost assuredly lose any chance to make a sale.

Instead, say you respect his relationship, and then ask about the specifics of the types of products and services a client already receives from his current supplier. Offer to do a comparison or evaluation of your client's current situation to see if you can identify areas where you can improve his situation. Allstate Insurance has long offered a "free" insurance evaluation to prospects as a way to encourage them to visit the Allstate Service Centers in Sears department stores. This approach must be very effective because Allstate has done it for decades.

Next, to raise doubts about the prospect's feeling of satisfaction, note one or more of the several problems that can arise from adopting a single-source approach. Here are some examples:

- Putting all your eggs in one basket can be dangerous: strikes, bankruptcies, buyouts, mergers, business failures, and the like, can disrupt the flow of goods and services you need.

- You cannot accurately judge quality and service unless you have more than one source.
- You may want to experiment with or test our products and services to compare the results we give you with those you get from our competitor's products and services.

Even if this approach does not work at first, keep trying. One survey has shown that almost half of every 1,000 purchasing agents leave their current jobs during any given twelve-month period. The more things change in selling, the more they change. In consumer selling, remember, too, that almost 20 percent of all families move every year, and need new services and stores. This peculiarly American mobility offers plenty of risk in that you often lose customers. But it also offers plenty of opportunity to gain new ones.

"I HAVE A BETTER OFFER"

Again, this is similar to the price concern, and you must ask for specifics and use the Big Picture to offset that concern. Here are probes you might use to find out how to offset or answer these concerns:

- Could you explain to me something about the other offer?
- What exactly appealed to you about the other offer?
- Perhaps you misunderstood my offer. Let's compare the other offer with the details of my complete package and see where we end up.
- You indicated you have talked to other vendors besides my company. May I ask what they offered and how it differs from ours?

"NO ONE HAS EVER ASKED FOR YOUR PRODUCT"

This is especially common when you're selling products to retailers, and it's similar to the "I've never heard of your product (company service, etc.)" concern. For both, respond with details about your company and its financial strength and stability, add testimonials of your product's success with other clients, refer the prospect to satisfied clients in his area or who he may know, use any supporting market research that forecasts favorable results for your product or service in the customer's industry, or, in consumer selling, present advantages. "Be the first on your block to own your very own Gizmo" has been effective for generations because it appeals to people's inherent desires to be unique, own something before anyone else does, increase their social prestige, get a step up on the neighbors, and so forth.

"I DON'T WANT TO CHANGE"

There are dozens of variations on this theme. It implies that the client fears change and the unknown. Emphasize benefits and offer reassurance. For example, suppose your client is thinking about buying a new car, but really likes his used one. When you probe, you may find out that his beloved old car has begun to break down more and more often.

You may respond: "It appears you've had a lot of trouble with your old car during the past six months. That must be very inconvenient and costly. So far, the car has not broken down in a dangerous situation, but it could, and that could harm your spouse and children. If you buy our model, you will have more legroom and a more comfortable ride, and you'll have our thirty-six-month guarantee. If anything happens, just bring it in and we'll fix it and give you a low-cost loaner until we get it fixed. With our extended warranty service, you even get the free towing up to twenty-five miles away from our dealership. You'll save time, worry, inconvenience and hassle."

Again, you are helping create a conflict in the buyer's mind, and showing him how to resolve that conflict in a satisfactory way.

"I HAD A BAD EXPERIENCE WITH A SIMILAR PRODUCT"

A client could also say he had a previous bad experience with your product, your company, your service, a different salesperson, and so forth. People tend to automatically reject your approach if they have had trouble in a similar situation. Your response should be to sympathize with the client's situation, without accepting or placing blame. Then, probe for the details of what happened. If the trouble just happened or continues, consider how you can help resolve it for the customer. Ask your client how he would like the situation to be corrected, improved, or prevented in the future.

Above all, do not deny the problem; even if your client has made it all up or lives in a fantasy world, the problem remains very real to *him*, and his feeling is the key, not the truth or falsehood of his accusation.

If the trouble occurred with your company, you should discuss how the situation, product line, service procedures, and so forth, have been improved. Put your efforts toward first creating a positive doubt in your client's mind. You want your client to think: "Perhaps things have changed for the better. They were good once, before they messed up that time. Maybe they can do it again."

Then work hard to re-establish your company's reputation and image with your client. Be very careful to take special care of these clients. If you do re-establish the relationship and then another serious mistake occurs, you will undoubtedly lose this client for good.

"WHAT IF SOMETHING HAPPENS?"

This concern expresses anxiety and clients want to be shown how to feel more confident in their decisions, especially when others review or oversee their decisions. Use testimonials and positive case histories to build confidence. Emphasize warranty, service policies and procedures, refer prospects to existing clients in similar situations, and speak in a soothing, reassuring tone of voice.

You may try general reassurances, such as, "Most of my clients have been pleased with their results," but this approach is not advisable if a client expresses serious reservations. Only more specific examples and references will impart the high level of assurance they require.

WHEN <u>NO</u> REALLY MEANS <u>NO!</u>

Of course, despite your best efforts, often "no" means just that and nothing you can say or do can change it. But any "no" is just temporary. Never interpret *No* as *Never,* but rather interpret it as *Not Now.* Then, don't waste the client's time or yours. Quickly, yet politely, end the interview. Be sure to stay in touch; remember that buyers often change positions, and circumstances in your own company and those of your competitors change, too. Today's competitor could become tomorrow's bankrupt. It could change its line of business. The competing salesperson could have a personality clash with the client, or the client could have a sudden need for product your competitor cannot fulfill. Any number of changes can shift the advantage in your direction at any time.

In short, stay in touch. Call again, probe for changed situations, send literature about new products, send the client clippings of articles or information in which he may have a direct interest. Persist!

FIVE-STEP "EMPHATIC EMPATHY" METHOD: OVERTURN OBJECTIONS IN YOUR FAVOR

Despite the seemingly innumerable concerns and objections clients can raise, you need follow only one process to respond to them all, the Emphatic Empathy Method. The purpose of this tactic is to turn each concern into a selling benefit. It consists of five steps. Using it, you may find selling easier and more pleasant than if you continued to use outdated ways to beat down objections.

STEP 1: LISTENING WITH EMPATHY

Let each client know by your words, deeds, and body language that you want to walk with him through the problem and work together to find a solution. Use your new listening techniques to hear between the lines to uncover the real objection.

STEP 2: SEE THE CONCERN THROUGH YOUR CLIENT'S EYES

An extension of empathy, this helps you understand that any client faces an element of uncertainty about any purchase. Even the most experienced buyer has some concern or anxiety about loss, change, failure, or difficulty before he makes a decision. The internal conflict can get out of hand and paralyze the buyer unless you empathize and reassure him.

STEP 3: AGREE WITH THE CLIENT'S FEELINGS

In traditional selling, the "Yes, but" approach has been used for years, but in consultative selling, if it is used too often, it smacks of an uncaring or flippant attitude. Avoid the quick response to make points and avoid starting an argument. Instead, adjust your posture to show understanding. Pause and consider which feelings your client's objection expresses. Then respond to those feelings.

During any of the first three steps, you can also repeat the objection to make sure both of you are on the same wavelength. Repeating the objection lets your client know you are listening, gives you time to think through your response, and helps calm the client.

Say something like, "Before I respond, let me make sure I understand exactly what you mean." Then you can ask a clarifying or fact-finding question to gain more specific information about an indefinite or vague objection.

In fact, it is better to avoid trying to respond to indefinite objections with a definite answer; you are shooting at a moving target. Instead, empathize with the feeling, and ask for more information. For example, "I understand your concern about making a change now. Could you tell me what specific concerns you have about changing vendors?"

STEP 4: MATCH THE MOOD

In many cases, a customer will act defensively or display hostility. People often do this to avoid showing anxiety or fear.

In such situations, act calmly and allow your client to save face and back off from his defensive or hostile posture. Remove yourself from the situation and use case histories, testimonials—the specific or general third-party lead-in to defuse the situation.

STEP 5: RAISE CONCERNS BEFORE YOUR CLIENT DOES

If you have done your homework, or you have a long-standing relationship, you may know what is of concern to your client most often, or you can at least anticipate it. Do this delicately, and avoid confronting likely concerns head-on. *Never* respond to a "fear" concern before it is raised. Confine your anticipatory presentation to anecdotes, analogies, parables, case histories, and the like. They allow a client to think for himself and come to his own understanding of your presentation.

Notice that these five steps do not follow traditional lines. They treat questioning and the F/A/B approach as adjuncts to the main purpose: discovering and exploring a client's feelings and attitudes.

REACH A CONSENSUS

After you follow this process, how can you show your clients you honestly and thoroughly understand their concerns? How, and when, can you ease toward a close? The best time is: When you reach a "consensus" with your client. This consensus is simply a verbal or written agreement that both you and your client have identified the situation, agreed on the exact nature of his problems, needs, or concerns, and uncovered the most likely reasons for them. When you reach consensus, you can easily offer your solutions to his problems and move toward a final close.

You may have to reach consensus several times during a sales call, as you work through each concern. But always before you try an incremental close, reach consensus about the most immediate concern. Otherwise, you may easily fall into contention and misunderstanding.

If you carefully reach consensus, your client will feel that he has been treated with respect. He will feel that you appreciate his situation, and you have worked together to solve his problems in partnership.

Use these statements to begin a consensus:

- I believe you are saying your key concerns are . . .
- If I may sum up our discussion, the main points we've explored include . . .
- If I understand you correctly, you are saying . . .

You may end your description of the consensus with a question, such as:

- Are we agreed that these are your main concerns?
- Have I identified your problem as you understand it?
- Have we zeroed in on the situation as it exists today?
- Do you think I've adequately summarized your needs?

Using questions like these will allow your client another opportunity to finalize his thoughts and will help you and him clarify any lingering doubts or misconceptions. Above all, the consensus accomplishes one overriding objective: understanding the real need, the Hinge, before presenting your solution.

Now, all you need do is apply the Handle—your solutions to the client's problems—to open the door to a sale.

Chapter 7

HANDLES ON SUCCESS

Consultative Closing Techniques

Moving toward a close in consultative selling becomes a logical outcome of the consensus you and your client reach. In fact, it should be almost anticlimactic, the result of a deliberate and mutually beneficial process. During that process, you and your client will have identified his real—not hyped or created—needs or desires, considered how your product or service can best meet those needs, and demonstrated through a sales effort, demonstration, or pilot program how your company's offer does accomplish that goal. A successful close results when the buyer agrees that your products will meet his requirements better than any other available and places an order.

This model works well in theory and often in practice, but the real world tends to throw enough curves to keep everyone hopping. Neither buyers nor sellers have perfect knowledge, and often, people buy to meet emotional needs, not actual needs. That is why, in consultative selling, you need to understand feelings and emotional reactions and how to fulfill them more than you need to understand your own products and services. Of course, you must understand these, too. But, except when absolute technical accuracy is required in the selling role, your knowledge of human emotional reactions will have more meaning.

Yet, in closing a sale, you cannot get too caught up in a client's emotional trauma: his reluctance to make a commitment, his remaining doubts, any problems he might have with his relationship to his own job and company. In consultative selling, salespeople fail most often because they forget the cardinal rule of selling: You still must ask the buyer to buy. You can ask questions, listen intently, answer objections, and empathize all day long, but unless you ask a buyer to sign on the dotted line and part with his cash, you cannot succeed.

TURN THE SALES HANDLE TO CLOSE

Closing a sale means you simply ask someone to do what he already wants to do, that is, obtain a product, service, or result that will satisfy his physical and emotional needs and desires. In other words, closing the sale means you turn the Sales Handle to move the customer's Hinge. To do that, you create a set of circumstances—your offer and his reactions— that will relieve the client's inner conflict.

In the past, traditional selling considered the "close" to be a tactic or game of tug-of-war in which the salesperson tried to drag the prospect across a line called "buy now" while the prospect tried to drag the salesperson across a line called "not now," or, more often, "make concessions." This point of view created the adversarial relationship between buyers and sellers. As discussed in the previous chapter, buyers are reluctant to commit to a purchase because they fear loss, misunderstand the situation, react with too much anxiety, or cannot act because of outside pressures. None of these or other legitimate reasons for a buyer's hesitance are mysterious or unknowable; you can find them out with your probing techniques. But what about the salesperson? There are those who are afraid to ask for the order. If you are one of these, then the next section is for you.

FEAR OF CLOSING— AND HOW TO OVERCOME IT

When salespeople fear closing, the reasons are often simple to understand. Here are a number of the common fears, signs by which you can recognize them in yourself, and tactics by which you can overcome them.

RELUCTANCE TO APPLY PRESSURE

In many cases, valid reasons exist to avoid applying pressure to close. One is that the salesperson believes it would jeopardize a carefully constructed relationship. However, salespeople walk a fine line. Buyers in most circumstances want and expect to be asked to buy. In new, deregulated industries, especially banking and financial services, the traditional, pinstriped banker may feel that he is a banker first and a salesperson second. But now, personal bankers, even new account officers and tellers, face the challenge of discovering the needs of their current customers for additional financial services and learning how to prospect for new customers to sell services they may not have considered before. In this case, the salesperson must overcome his own self-image and the client's reluctance to accept the new image.

Even if you are not in financial sales, you might find yourself reluctant to ask for the order. To overcome this problem, work on your self-image. Get help if need be, but work at convincing yourself that you are, indeed, performing a valuable service—and need not fear asking for what *you* need at the end of it, an order.

IGNORANCE OF <u>HOW</u> TO CLOSE

Some salespeople just may not know how to close in a consultative manner in a particular situation. If you feel this way, study the rest of this chapter and ask your management for additional training in how to close.

For example, one new, young sales representative for a national adhesives company found that even after three months of training, he still expected customers to offer to buy simply because he had given an exceptional presentation. He sat back and waited for the orders to roll in. It did not work that way. He learned eventually that the orders did come more readily when he began to simply ask for them.

IGNORANCE OF <u>WHEN</u> TO CLOSE

More specifically, however, the same young salesperson said he did not recognize buying signals and talked his way out of several sure sales by talking too much and listening and watching too little. He learned a key closing principle: Close Early and Often. In other words, he now asks closing questions at various stages of the sales call. Failing to recognize closing signals *and* act on them are the most common reasons salespeople do not close.

FEAR OF ACCEPTANCE AND SUCCESS

Although it may seem odd to many to mention fear of success, noted psychologists have found that fear of success probably forms the second most important reason for failing to close. The RET (Rational Emotive Therapy) school of psychotherapy, led by Albert Ellis, explains that success can attack a person's underlying negative self-image and force him to come to grips with an unaccustomed and frightening positive self-image. When faced with a significant threat to their negative self-image, people generally pull back or sabotage their successful action. How better to sabotage yourself than by failing to close a sale?

Success can also cause the monster of perfectionism to raise its demanding head. Many salespeople believe—falsely—that they *must* succeed. If they have succeeded before, they must always succeed, or they will be terrible people. This grandiose thinking is very unrealistic and very self-defeating because everyone succeeds and fails in various measure all the time. But if he fails to close a sale, even if he has absolutely no control over the situation, many a salesperson will use this failure to confirm and reinforce his fundamentally negative self-image.

Other reasons for fear of success Ellis describes include a dire need to be loved or approved and a low level of frustration tolerance, to name two. Ellis notes that people often tell themselves: "I expect to fail, and I can tolerate that, therefore

I must fail. If I succeed, how can I ever tolerate less than success again?"

If you recognize that you have a negative self-image, or make unrealistic demands on yourself, you need to recognize the truth of Ellis' common sense advice: you *can* accept yourself as a person regardless of your success or failure as a salesperson. Once you've done that, you're less likely to pin your whole life on every closing. You'll relax about it, and finally get down to business without even thinking about it.

Everyone succeeds and fails in various endeavors; some succeed more often than others in different ways. One person sells 13,000 cars a year, another sells only a few hundred, another sells none. That third person may not sell automobiles well, but that does not make him a failure as a person. He needs to re-evaluate his desire to sell cars, and obtain more training, find something he likes to sell better, or change his career. These are reasonable and realistic responses to fear of failure.

FEAR OF REJECTION

Many people become involved in sales because they like to be with other people. Salespeople are usually a very gregarious group and they like other people and they like other people to approve of them. They tend to have higher than average needs for approval, and they tend to like to please others. And, far more than the general public believes, salespeople see themselves as servants who sincerely want to help their clients. They regard their clients as friends and want to help these people get what they want. In fact, the characteristics of the consistently spectacular and successful salespeople show that they are the ones who make finding and satisfying their customer's emotional needs their top priority.

They are also in constant and intimate contact with their companies, the products they sell, and their clients, so it is very easy—and very human—for salespeople to blur the distinctions between their sales efforts and themselves. They tend to feel worse about rejection than many other types of people do. They find it hard to separate their self-image from their sales pitch. But you must separate the two and understand that *you* are not being rejected, only your proposal is, when you fail to get the order.

Ellis strongly advises practicing "unconditional self-acceptance," that is, you would do best to accept yourself as a worthy, deserving person just because you exist. The basic premise of RET is that no person can be condemned as a person for what he or she is; one may criticize or condemn another person's *actions,* or what they do, but not who they *are.*

Everyone has at least a small dose of fear of rejection. That is healthy and can spur you to make a better sales presentation. But you need to face and cope with any deep anxiety that prevents you from making sales calls or closing a sale. Here's how:

First, never take a rejection as a personal insult.

Second, identify and prevent the numerous games you can play to keep yourself from closing a sale. Most often, people concentrate on the presentation and "forget" to close. They do not "hear" or they may even ignore clear buying signals. They emphasize listening and responding to clients' objections, instead of using objections to close the sale. They make unnecessary sales calls on current, satisfied customers so they can avoid making calls on new prospects. They spend most of their time making presentations to staff members who cannot make buying decisions. In short, they procrastinate and find dozens of subtle ways to indefinitely delay the risk of rejection. But they also delay the prospect of success.

Here are several other ways to cope—successfully—with a fear of rejection:

1. Adopt the "no pain, no gain" principle. In sports, an athlete cannot improve his performance without exerting effort, effort that is often painful and may even fail to achieve the desired result. Salespeople do the same thing when they improve their sales performances by making one more cold call, or asking for the sale just one more time. Each time you

ask, you will add strength to your sales muscle and your resolve.

2. Build success into every sales call. Adopt an attitude that *you* will not be turned down, even if the buyer does not buy.

Structure into your presentation a small series of successes for yourself, even if your proposal is rejected in the end. Your questions will help you; each time you get a positive response to any level of the probing, you will have experienced some success. And, when you create good feelings in the client's mind, you give yourself a boost, too.

3. Avoid preoccupation with gaining the client's personal approval. If you urgently need a client's personal acceptance, you may fear you will insult him or harm your relationship by closing the sale. Ellis would add that you tell yourself another key erroneous thought: you first tell yourself you desperately need the client's approval, and then, to make matters worse, you tell yourself that it will be an awful, terrible thing—an act that damages your soul—if the client rejects your proposal. Ellis says that you must dispute with yourself the notion that rejection is so awful as to be unbearable. Regard it as merely inconvenient, and go on.

Concentrate on accepting yourself as a worthy, deserving person because you are who you are.

4. Above all, stick to your primary purpose: showing the client how to best satisfy his needs, solve his problems, or gain desirable benefits by using your products and services. Your purpose is not and never will be to gain the personal approval of your clients.

5. Finally, accept rejection as a *temporary* fact of life. As discussed in previous chapters, buyers have as many reasons for rejecting a sales pitch as for accepting one. See one rejection as a temporary situation that, in all likelihood, time and changed circumstances may turn to your favor. If you fear rejection and worry about it, you could easily refuse to call on that prospect again—and miss a new selling opportunity when the buying pendulum swings toward you.

Following these steps, you can turn a reasonable fear of rejection into a personal strength, and you can either neutralize a serious fear of rejection, or ease its crushing power over your efforts. Ask any successful person if they have known defeat. You will be graced with a knowing smile. Truly successful salespeople, however, learn from their defeats. They see any rejection as a chance to improve or correct their presentations. And they are almost always eager to return to the fray.

LACK OF FAITH IN THE PRODUCT

Some salespeople do not really believe in the products or services they sell, and therefore have a very hard time asking someone else to invest money in them. Ideally, companies hire only committed, enthusiastic salespeople. But actually, they do not. Salespeople seek the wrong jobs, are hired for the wrong reasons, or just do not ever get into the swing of things with their employers. Or a once-good relationship between the seller and his company sours, and he loses the faith he once had. If this is the case, obviously, the salesperson needs to find a better job, and sales management needs to determine whether the salesperson could benefit from counseling, retraining, reassignment, or dismissal. Both management and the individual will be happier if the situation changes.

Signs of a lack of faith include:

- Boredom, usually obvious because the rest of the sales team seems to be working with normal enthusiasm and commitment.
- Declining sales over a period of months or several quarters, with no other explanation, such as stronger competition, an economic downturn, or assignment to a smaller or more difficult territory.
- Overt disenchantment with the company, such as abnormal complaints about working conditions, salary, etc.

If you recognize similar symptoms in yourself, you could be doing your company and yourself a disservice by continuing in the same role.

RECOGNIZE AND CLOSE ON BUYING SIGNALS

Most salespeople experience a normal fear of rejection and cope with it as well as can be expected. Often more difficult for salespeople to correct is their failure to recognize and act upon a client's buying signals. Yet, how often have you heard someone, or even yourself, say, with some exasperation, "The customer did not say he wanted to buy. I thought he was listening to what I had to say."

As explained in Chapter 5, the best salespeople listen far more often than they talk, usually in a ratio of 70–30, listening to talking. Salespeople listen not only to *hear* a client's emotional reactions, but also to *see* how he expresses those reactions in his body language. More often than not, salespeople are not well acquainted with physical buying signals. Fortunately, recognizing "buying body language" is as easy and simple as following the traffic laws at a railroad track: STOP, LOOK, and LISTEN. Good salespeople stop talking, start watching, and always keep listening. With 70 percent of the time you spend in each sales call—42 minutes per hour—you have plenty of time to understand what your client is telling you and relate his verbal message to his physical one.

Remember to adopt an interested body posture of your own. Sit forward in your chair, lean toward the buyer, fold your hands on your lap, look steadily at the buyer, and wait patiently for him to answer your questions or explain his point of view. Then watch and listen for these and similar buying signals.

TEN VERBAL SIGNALS

Here are ten common spoken signals that tell you the customer is ready to buy:

1. Asking whether your product will help him do something, accomplish some objective, or execute some task.

2. Asking about price, even if it is a price concern or objection. A statement like "We cannot afford it at this time"

may show a desire to buy if you can satisfy his concern about price.

3. Asking about any discounts, deals, promotions, or special deals you may offer or that you discussed during your presentation.

4. Asking about profit margins from reselling your product to the public.

5. Asking about specific benefits from using your product.

6. Querying terms and conditions. This often indicates a need for reassurance and signals an acceptance of your product's advantages and benefits.

7. Asking comparative questions about what the client has now and what you are offering, or between what you offer and what another seller offers.

8. Asking for references to or the names of other companies that use your product, or for information about how other companies are using it.

9. Asking where in his store, plant, factory, facility, home, yard, automobile, etc., your product might best be installed or how your service can be put to best use.

10. Asking about return policies, warranties, guarantees, delivery, and service policies. This is the most explicit buying signal there is. Your client has made the emotional shift and now has a picture in his mind of how he or his company can use your product.

If you hear these or any similar questions or comments, move quickly to satisfy the immediate concern and ask the buyer to buy.

NINETEEN PHYSICAL SIGNALS

As important as spoken signals are the unspoken signals expressed by a buyer's body language. Watch for these signals, particularly when you are edging toward a close and in response to your questions. Be sure, too, to consider body signals in concert or combination with spoken signals. Buyers may know the principles of body language, but it will take an expert prevaricator to cover up all his intentions. If you see conflicting signals, be very alert. Either your client is confused and uncertain, or he is trying to disguise a reaction. Probe further any time you recognize conflicting spoken and physical signals.

Here are sets of physical signals that indicate your client's negative or positive reactions:

Nine Negative Buying Signals

1. The Lips Don't Like It. While many salespeople watch people's eyes, you would do better to watch their lips. A client is saying "no" with tight lips, lips pressed against his teeth, or with pursed lips. Fortunately for you, emotional reactions almost always find expression in lip movements, far more so than in the eyes or the body. When you see "no, no" lips, find out what has caused the customer to act hostilely immediately. Except in love, "yes, yes" eyes mean very little.

2. Tossing It Off. Picking up a brochure or leaflet and tossing it aside or flicking it down indicates displeasure and dismissal.

3. Who's Licked Now? Not you, not yet. But licking the lips does show fear, and demands that you reassure this client and ease his anxiety.

4. Hot Potatoes. Handling anything connected with your presentation hesitantly as if it were "too hot to handle" shows a client does not want to be associated with your product.

5. Cat on a Hot Tin Roof. Making nervous, jerky gestures shows your client has something on his mind he is not expressing.

6. Magic Acts. Pointing one's shoulder toward you, coupled with leaning back and crossing the arms, means your client wants you to disappear. He wants to dismiss you from his thoughts.

7. Peek-a-Boo. Refusing to look at you straight-on or eye-to-eye may show timidity, fear of disappointing you and your

subsequent disapproval of him, or a wish to avoid facing the situation. Flicking side glances at you or in your direction shows similar reactions.

8. Getting the Gate. Pushing things on a desk toward you and away from himself implies your client wants to disassociate himself from you or for you to leave.

9. Out, Out Damn Spot. Flicking anything—dust, lint, ashes, dirt, or something imaginary—from his clothing also implies dismissal. He is flicking your offer away from him and creating distance between you.

Ten Positive Buying Signals

1. The Lips Like It. Positive lip signals are more pleasant to see. A slight, warm smile, lips upturned at the corners, or relaxed lips all show a good reaction to you and a willingness to hear more, if not a wish to close now.

2. Paper Fondling. Picking up and laying down a leaflet or brochure politely or gently shows the buyer respects your presentation and will entertain your offer.

3. Play It Again, Sam. Repeatedly looking through or studying your order form. This indicates serious interest in the details and a desire to buy. Stop talking and wait patiently for your client to continue as he studies your literature or order form.

4. Nosing Around. Stepping back, walking back toward or appraising your sample or demonstration a second, third, or subsequent time shows strong interest. It may also show a desire for reassurance, so use case histories, testimonials, or confidence-builders to give him that feeling.

5. Picking Winners. Showing you, handling, or pointing toward his own choice of model, size, shape, or color means the buyer has made the mental shift to a point at which he is already using or experiencing your product or service.

6. Expectant Father Syndrome. Rising from a chair and pacing back and forth means the buyer is seriously considering your proposition. NEVER interrupt someone who paces.

7. Searching for Backers. Looking at or toward a partner, superior, or supportive employee means your client is looking for support for a decision he has made or is about to make. Give him that support he seeks and close.

8. Buying Into the Deal. In retail situations, looking around your store as if he were counting inventory shows the buyer has decided to become personally involved with you and wants to know more about you or gain reassurance.

9. Fingers Do the Talking. Searching for a notepad or paper on which to jot figures or calculate numbers. Also reaching for a purchase order or requisition form, or operating a calculator. Your client is on the mental verge of buying.

10. The Land of Plenty. Pulling out an inventory sheet, checking stock levels, calling for definite information from a subordinate means you have created a doubt in your client's mind as to whether the current supply is adequate, and he may want to buy more to have reassurance. You need to move toward a close and couch it in terms of replenishing inventory or making sure he has enough on hand to meet the factory's needs.

As you watch and listen, follow the simple five-step process of recognizing and satisfying your client's emotional needs. Recognize your client's feelings, identify the source of any concerns or negative feelings, satisfy the concern, turn the negative feeling into a positive one, and ask for the sale.

A BAKER'S DOZEN CONSULTATIVE CLOSES

Recognizing buying signals still does not bring you any closer to actually asking the buyer to buy. Nor does all the self-assessment in the world, unless you know a few ways to conduct a close. But, like the young person who had trouble closing, you will still need to close early and often to reach your goals.

Here are a baker's dozen closing techniques. Blend them if you like to suit the stage of your presentation and the reaction of your client.

THE ASSUMPTIVE CLOSE

In consultative selling, the assumptive close is the most desirable and easiest one. With this, your client has truly sold himself on your product. If you have reached the desired consensus with your client and have presented your best solutions, often you can simply assume your client wants to close the sale and so take steps to make a formal agreement. This close works on several psychological bases. First, your client sees that your products fulfill his needs. Second, people will often do what you *expect* them to do. And third, you have conditioned your client to accept your offer.

To use an assumptive close, concentrate on details of the purchase: delivery, credit terms, discounts, installation, implementation, and so forth. Combine the dry facts with reassurances: "We can deliver your new loveseat on Thursday. I'm sure your friends who plan to visit on Saturday will love it. From what I understand of your decor, it should look smashing." You assume the customer wants to close, and appeal to her need for approval and pride in showing off her new acquisition.

THE TESTIMONIAL CLOSE

The testimonial close comes in very handy in consultative selling. You must constantly reassure clients, ease their fears, and relieve their anxieties. A testimonial close, also called an anecdotal or case history close, gathers evidence to support your claims. This helps ease a client's fear of making errors. These closes let the client feel that "if Joe at ABC liked it, it must be okay." They also create a "we're all in this together" feeling. Instead of just repeating a testimonial or giving a successful example, emphasize the benefits the other client received. For example, "Joe Jones at Jones, Jones, and Jones

CPAs bought our personal computer with XYZ spreadsheet and saved $50,000 a year in timesharing costs and increased his staff's productivity 50 percent."

THE STUMBLING BLOCK CLOSE

Use this close to overcome one major obstacle preventing the close. This is especially useful in consultative selling because you can easily resolve minor or small differences with questions, listening, and the F/A/B approach. With this, isolate the single most important problem and concentrate on solving it. The stumbling block may be fear, price, terms, or just about anything else. But when it is identified, you can zero in on it, and avoid any secondary distractions.

THE PRESENTATION CLOSE

Any time you conduct a successful "test drive" of your product, even if a client only handles a sample and appears to like it, lead directly into an agreement. Do not wait until the end of a presentation, demonstration, test drive, pilot program, or sample use; as soon as the product appears to gain a buyer's approval, ask the buyer to buy. "Mr. Smith, you appear to like how our new X-2000 model handles. And you look terrific behind the wheel, and Mrs. Smith seems to like it too. Let's go back to the showroom and draw up a contract right now."

You want to take advantage of your client's current enthusiasm and reinforce the good feelings he has experienced by participating in the "test drive." Those good feelings often override any minor concerns that inevitably crop up and seem to loom large if the client has time to worry about them.

THE SUCCESSION CLOSE

This method, also called a minor decision or series of agreements close, works through a series of minor decisions to lead directly to a major purchasing decision. Work through a series of already accepted or acceptable points and then ask for a definite buying decision. For example, "Isn't this new front-wheel drive car more comfortable than your old car? It seems especially comfortable for the kids because the hump in the floorboard is gone, doesn't it? It should double your gas mileage, save on maintenance costs, and save the time you're spending repairing your old car. And don't you think our trade-in offer is more than what you thought we'd offer? Wouldn't you agree that buying your car now is wiser than throwing good money after bad?" By the time a client has said "yes" several times, he may be ready to say "yes" the one, most important time, too.

THE ALTERNATIVES CLOSE

This close encourages your client to make choices and, in doing so, make a firm commitment to buy. It can be risky in consultative selling unless you correctly gauge your client's state of mind. Giving a client a choice could open the door to his making the wrong choice or saying no. Confine the alternatives you present to product or service features, delivery schedules, or terms and conditions. Here are some examples:

- Would you prefer to handle your electronic funds transfers in the morning or the afternoon?
- Do you prefer our no-interest, three-payment plan or our regular monthly payment plan?

Never present a "yes or no" to the entire sale during an alternatives close.

THE "OURS VERSUS THEIRS" CLOSE

Also known as the comparative close, use this one carefully and avoid denigrating a competitor's product. It may be best to avoid this kind of close if your client already uses a competing product. It appears unwise to bring the competition to mind as you move to close a sale. It appears more appropriate to confine such comparisons to the F/A/B portion of the sales call.

Support any "ours versus theirs" close with third party or outside objective supporting evidence. Say, for example, "You may know the XYZ widget has a quality rating of 10, but tests by the respected and objective Commercial Testing Laboratory show that our widget has a quality rating of 25. And our current clients say that our superior quality saves them 15 percent of the costs of reworking their products. How many would you like today?"

THE IMPASSIVE CLOSE

If your client acts like an oyster—he's hard to get out of his shell—use this close after you have made a successful presentation and attempted several other closes. It requires mere patience.

Ask for the sale, sit back, relax, look the customer in the eye, and wait for him to speak up. This can be risky, of course, and can best be attempted when you believe your client is delaying or stalling or trying to exact concessions you are not willing to give. Ask direct questions, such as, "When do you want us to deliver your order?" and "It seems you need quite a large order. How many thousands do you need?" And then wait—for an answer or an indication that you need to cover some ground again, and then try another close.

THE "HOOK" CLOSE

This approach compels the buyer to act now. Use it in consultative selling when you can offer an exceptional promotion, special offer, discount, or extra. "Mr. James, it appears you are a little low on inventory. Right now, we have a special offer. We will pay freight charges and give you a dozen free boxes if you order 200 boxes now. You can replenish your inventory and avoid having to order when industry-wide prices are scheduled to go up in the next quarter."

THE "GIVE-IN" CLOSE

Also called a concession close, it is the kissing cousin of the hook close. It means you give your client something he wants, preferably a relatively minor point, if he agrees to buy. "Yes, we can make sure you receive your shipment on the same day each month. That will help smooth out your production runs and make your process more efficient. Now, how many widgets do you want to order?"

THE FEAR CLOSE

With this close, take one of several approaches:

1. Show your client that he can ease his fear of losing something by buying your product.

2. Show that your client's fear may worsen, and he could lose even more than he has if he does not act and buy your product. This is effective when someone already faces a bad situation and is searching for, if not a clean solution, at least a way out of the worst.

3. Show your client the good feelings he will experience by buying your product. Emphasize benefits, positive future experiences, pleasant results, and advantages your client will gain with your products. For example, "If you buy a microcomputer now, you can save $250 on your 1986 taxes. With a little training, you will present to your boss better, more accurate, more easily understood reports than he has ever received. Your boss will certainly appreciate the improvement, and you will have a step up on others still using pencil and paper."

If you doubt that this approach works, consider that Visi-Corp. sold 500,000 copies of its VisiCalc™ spreadsheet for two reasons: it saved middle managers enormous amounts of drudgery, and it gave a professional, competitive advantage to the manager or professional who installed one in his office first.

The "fear" close is often used in various traditional consultative industries: insurance, funeral services, tax accounting,

accounting, management consulting, market research, and many more. In consumer selling, it is most often used to satisfy the very real emotion of vanity and the accompanying fear people have that they appear unattractive to others. The apparel, cosmetics, diet, exercise, cosmetic surgery, and similar industries rest on that foundation.

THE SUMMARY CLOSE

This is an excellent and appropriate consultative close. It flows directly from the consensus you and your client reach. Reiterate what you see as the Hinge (the client's needs or problem), explain to him the key benefits of your product or service (the Handle), and ask for the order.

Here's an example:

"As I understand it, your company needs a high quality, reliable source of black and blue carpets. We make 1,000 yards of black and blue carpet each year and we have for fifteen years. With just two weeks' notice, we can easily increase our production run if you need a greater quantity. According to the Carpet Testing Institute, our nylon B&B IV carpet is the highest quality carpet available in that material and style. And we have averaged less than 1 percent late deliveries to our customers for the past ten years. Would you like deliveries to start in two weeks?"

THE STRAIGHTFORWARD CLOSE

Of course, in many consultative situations, where your relationships are firm or your client is very open about his needs, you simply ask a straight question, that is, "Ma'am, we want your business, and I want to work with you. Can we consider this a deal?"

Develop your own applications for each of these closes, and you will be well prepared to recognize your client's buying signals and move quickly, smoothly, and successfully to close the sale.

Chapter 8

KEYS TO THE KINGDOM

Essential Client Support Techniques for Future Sales

Perhaps the most overlooked "secret" of consultative selling can be summed up in one word: cultivation. Like crops that wither from lack of watering, weeding, and transplanting, the "fruit" of your labor will wither on the vine if you do not cultivate it. What is this fruit? The relationship you establish with each client. Although your primary purpose in consultative selling is to fulfill your clients' needs, your personal goal must be to establish long-term, positive relationships between your firm and your clients.

You keep this goal in mind for both selfish and altruistic reasons. To put it selfishly, making repeat sales to satisfied customers takes less time, brings in more money, makes higher profits, and brings more pleasure to you than hoeing the hard row of cold calls and planting "seeds" to raise new prospects. Altruistically, making repeat sales allows the client to save time, act with more confidence, avoid bad feelings, and gain more pleasure from working with someone he knows and respects.

GAIN THE POWER OF REFERRALS
FROM SATISFIED CUSTOMERS

Most important for you, the salesperson, is that you are likely to obtain referrals from satisfied customers to whom you have made repeat sales. Everyone knows word-of-mouth advertising—both favorable and unfavorable—is the most powerful form of advertising there is. Why? Because buyers respond enthusiastically to recommendations from people they trust. The movie industry knows this. They know critics have little impact on whether or not a movie is popular, but the opinions of your neighbors, friends, co-workers, and relatives have a tremendous impact. Consider some of the highest grossing movies ever—*Star Wars*, *Rocky*, *Back to the Future*, and so on—and you will find that the critics either panned or were lukewarm toward all of them. People were not and the box office tallies tell the tale.

In essence, by cultivating a long-term relationship with each client, you encourage a word-of-mouth advertising campaign in your favor. Yet, most salespeople *never*—that's right, never—follow up on a sales call unless the buyer himself initiates the contact.

OVERCOME THE FEAR OF FOLLOW-THROUGH

Why don't salespeople follow up and establish these obviously worthwhile relationships? One reason and one reason only: fear. Fear that your client has a problem, fear that he does not like your product, fear that he wants you to take the product back but just has not got the courage to call you, and many other nerve-racking reasons. Such fears derive from insecurity and your lack of belief in yourself, your company, and your products.

If you have followed the Consultative Protocol, however, you have no need to be afraid. Such insecurities arise when you believe you have pulled a fast one on the buyer. If you have worked with the buyer, identified his needs, met those needs in a mutually agreeable manner, and helped the buyer sell himself, he will have little cause for complaint and you will have no reason for fear. How, in such a case, could you possibly have "pulled a fast one?" You could not, and did not, and the fears are shadows floating through your mind to pull you off the track.

So banish fear of follow-up from your mind. It has no place in consultative selling. In fact, consultative selling developed partially as a method to reduce the anxiety and conflict both buyers and sellers have long felt in selling situations. Consider which of these ways you would prefer to feel:

- Boy, I'm glad I squeezed that sale out. She really didn't like the color, and she was worried about the fit. Now, if the darned swimming suit holds together for thirty days, I'll be okay.

or

- I'm glad we both agreed she looks best in the tank suit style and bright solid colors. She's very happy, and I feel pretty good about it too. And it will take her at least through this season and part of next without going out of style. She may even want a second one later for variety.

Of course, you want to feel happy and secure, not worried, or even haunted about a bad result.

In sum, if your clients feel good about how they feel, their buying decisions, and their relationship with you, they will eagerly refer you to friends of theirs. When this happens, you may spend so much of your time making sales calls to referrals ready and willing to listen, you will reduce your cold calls and prospecting to almost nothing.

It's an amazingly simple and beautiful way to relieve salespeople's most dreaded task: prospecting for new customers. Your clients actually *pay* you to conduct an advertising campaign on your behalf, and they do it simply because they feel good about you and your relationship with them. If that is not the most ingenious selling system "never" invented, I don't know what is. And it was *never invented* because it grew from basic human relationships. It comes from a basic desire on the part of each person to willingly help someone whom they like or who has helped them.

CULTIVATE LONG-TERM
RELATIONSHIPS

Even better, cultivating relationships is easier, simpler, and more fun than making cold calls and prospecting. The process starts as soon as you close the sale. Although Paul Simon says there are fifty ways to leave your lover, there is only one good way to leave a client: on an upbeat note and with both of you in a positive frame of mind.

If you've made a sale, you may feel exuberant and want to rush out to celebrate or make your next call while you are "on a roll." Avoid this reaction because it may make your client feel ill-used and tossed aside. Instead, work to create a good impression and set the stage to take care of any details, such as delivery schedules or installation dates, and set a time and date for your next sales call.

Never leave any sales call, especially an unsuccessful one, without getting a commitment to follow through, provide more information, call again, something to keep the chance to establish a relationship alive. The classified advertising manager for a national publication says he insists that his staff get some commitment from the client for future interest. Set up another appointment, pin down a definite time you can call in the future, determine whether or not and what type of literature a client wants, something, anything—although you won't want to act desperately or rudely if a client is still not interested. In any case, thank the client, and show respect for his feelings. Remember that "no" now simply means a temporary delay in making a sale. And what you say as you leave an interview or hang up the telephone, and how you say it, simply make up the next step toward a successful close.

In successful sales calls, reassure your clients that they have acted intelligently and obtained for themselves and their companies the feelings they desire and a good solution to their problems. Above all, don't be in a hurry to leave. That may leave a sour taste and spoil any future business. Don't dawdle either; it's awkward and makes everyone feel uncomfortable. And buyers also have other things to do. Simply leave after the last details are covered, and you have properly, but not effusively, thanked your client.

ANALYZE YOUR RESULTS

As soon as practical after a sales call, analyze your results. Ask yourself not only what went wrong, but what went right. Do not dwell on the negative. Reinforce the positive. Someone once pointed out that you do, in fact, learn from losing: you learn how to lose. So instead, consider positive, analytical questions about what happened, such as:

- What did I say or do that most impressed this client?
- What positive feelings was I able to evoke for this client?
- In what ways was this client similar to or different from other clients?
- How can I use what I have learned to act more effectively in future sales calls?
- What have I learned about what people think, how they react and what they feel and believe about me, about my company, about my product, about themselves and about their situations?
- What have I learned about myself?

You can answer these questions in your head as you drive to the next appointment. Review what went right, then follow through, follow through, and follow through some more.

WEED OUT PROBLEMS BEFORE THEY TAKE HOLD

Within a few days or weeks after a sale, call your client. Never wait for problems to occur. Take a "pro-active" stance, as the jargoneers would say. Make sure your client enjoys his purchase and receives the benefits he had hoped for. If he does, reinforce his decision with a verbal pat on the back, and remind him of the step he took during your sales call that encouraged him to make his own decision. Then, if you can, tell him you are sending him a gift, an inexpensive, but not "cheap," small token of your appreciation. If possible, the gift should be directly related to the product he bought and add a little value to his decision.

Then, ask for referrals, not in such a direct manner, of course, but by saying something like this: "I wonder if you know anyone else who would appreciate my help." It's simple, and very, very effective.

This approach works wonders in any field. For example, one astute flower seller, parked by a roadside in south Florida, used this approach to plant his stand firmly in the minds of two new clients. After some hesitation at what appeared to be a high cost, the obviously Yuppie couple bought an expensive bunch of flowers. As money changed hands, the couple asked a question about the difficulty of doing business in that particular city. As the conversation continued, it appeared the seller and the couple shared many attitudes about local government. As the discussion wound down, and the couple started to leave, the flower seller gave the woman a free red carnation "to match her blouse." That led to a few more minutes' conversation, and then the flower seller gave the woman a red rose.

Does this meet the "specs" for excellent consultative follow-through, although this salesman was just selling flowers from an aged van on the side of a dusty road? You bet it does. Here's why:

- He recognized excellent prospects when he saw them; they both looked and acted as if they were accustomed to having a fair amount of discretionary income.
- He probed to find out what type of flowers they wanted to buy, and didn't push those he wanted to sell—although he did offer to bundle into the sale for a small extra

charge a less expensive bunch the man had his eye on marginally. But he did not press when they declined.

- He listened and answered their concerns about price and made a counteroffer that was actually not as appealing as the original price.

- He discovered which flowers would give the couple the best feelings, and helped them sell themselves on those flowers.

- He added value to the bunch by adding ferns and baby's breath and wrapped the flowers nicely.

- He responded to questions and explored common ground when he identified it, even when it only marginally concerned flowers.

- He made sure the couple was pleased with their purchase and helped them realize that they would enjoy it. "These beautiful flowers will last at least ten days, and the buds will bloom very well," he pointed out.

- He obtained a commitment from the couple to call again and promised he would be available when they needed more flowers.

- He sought their help in obtaining new clients, asking them if they had stopped at the previous kiosk on the site, whether a lot of their friends drove down that road, and reassured them that he intended to serve the area as it had not been served in over two years.

- He reaffirmed their decision and gave not one, but two inexpensive presents that added value to their purchase. Instead of one large bunch of flowers, the couple also had lovely bud vases on their desks.

- The couple felt good and enjoyed their purchase. The flower seller felt good because he made some money, he established two new customers, and he helped them feel good.

This flower seller—long hair, dilapidated van, and all—whether by instinct or experience, clearly understood how to sell consultatively far better than most trained salespeople.

WHAT TO DO IF A PROBLEM STILL APPEARS

Unfortunately, every after-sales call will not go smoothly. What do you do if your client is dissatisfied or his company has a problem with your product or service? Most salespeople mumble an apology and try to blame someone else. But that doesn't help.

Instead, avoid taking it personally, and seize the opportunity to help correct the problem. Help resolve the problem with as much energy and enthusiasm as you brought to the initial sale. Your clients will be surprised, if not overwhelmed, by your "unusual" reaction: you want to help, you treat them with respect, you want to understand their problem, you want to relieve them of their distress. This attitude is so unusual in selling that you can rest assured it will usually help lead to a solid and prosperous long-term relationship. If you will act promptly to correct the problem and act as if you want to make your client feel better, most will go out of their way to forgive and forget what happened.

UPDATE: THE KEY TO FUTURE SUCCESS

After you have spoken with your clients on the telephone or corresponded with them following the initial sale, you will make subsequent personal sales calls, not only to obtain repeat sales, but to cultivate the account. Use follow-through or cultivation calls to enhance your client relationships, obtain repeat sales, and create new sales by cross-selling your other products and services. But to maximize your time, plan all cultivation sales calls. Follow these steps to plan and conduct each cultivation call.

1. Fill out and then refer to call reports. These need be no more elaborate than a 3-x-5-inch notecard for each customer, but you can also use automated client management programs. The information you keep should note what the client buys, when he buys, what motivated the client to buy, how you have followed up, any problems you have solved, and any extra added-value gifts you have given him.

2. Study the call reports or company files for current information about the client's status, any changes in his company and so forth.

3. During the cultivation call, follow these steps:

   a. Review your relationship and the most recent purchase.

   b. Ask whether or not your client is satisfied with the benefits he has received.

   c. Ask about current conditions in the client's line of business.

   d. Ask about any problems or difficulties the client has with your products or services or related ones.

   e. Discuss any problems and LISTEN.

   f. Help the client work through or discover solutions.

   g. Make recommendations and LISTEN to his responses.

   h. Reach a consensus about the problem and the solutions you both agree upon.

   i. Agree on what action both will take to resolve the situation.

   j. Take any on-the-spot action you can, such as meeting with others in the client's company.

   k. Identify cross-selling opportunities, if the situation is appropriate.

   l. Explore these opportunities, following your Consultation Protocol and the F/A/B approach.

   m. Set up the next step, or make the next appointment.

   n. Take your leave in a professional, pleasing manner.

WEAR SEVERAL HATS FOR SUCCESSFUL SALES

When you follow through with your customers, you play various roles and fulfill various functions. The most important is that of *liaison* or troubleshooter with your company. Just as your firm may require you to act as a bill collector on occasion, your client may "require" you to act as his hand-holder or sounding board or liaison officer. You must act well in these roles, of course, but you must also perform several other significant functions. You will at times act as a:

Client "News" Service. Your client may rely on you for news and trends in your industry that directly affect him, his company's future and how he uses your products. Service professions, such as insurance, accounting, and law, have long recognized this. Many professional firms buy or publish client newsletters to keep their clients abreast of important changes in law, regulations, trends, and industry offerings. Fulfill the same role with each client. Spend the time to call or send a clipping or drop a note in the mail about events and changes that directly affect or hold great interest for your clients.

Personal Acquaintance. If not a friend, you will become a significant business acquaintance to your clients. The larger and more important the account, of course, the more likely you will become more closely associated with them. Believe it or not, many people have few personal friends whom they see frequently, and they often experience most of their interpersonal contact in commercial or business situations. This is as true of the harried housewife with three kids who wants to see a smile and hear a kind word at the corner grocery as it is of the business executive who works twelve hours a day, seven days a week.

The relationship differs in quality, breadth, and depth, but it exists nonetheless. Recognize this and cultivate a pleasant, but not intimate association with your clients.

"Modern" salespeople do not get personal enough with their clients. As you make several sales calls, you should begin to learn the names, birthdays, anniversaries, and special or meaningful events concerning your clients, their spouses and children, their superiors, and so forth. Keep track of them, remember them with greeting cards, and entertain your client and his spouse on occasion.

Including a client's spouse in any dinner or entertainment is very important because most spouses, male or female, rarely go out with their spouses for dinner, especially if the spouse works and they have children. But be careful not to presume in this area. It is often regarded as a courtesy—but not until after a fairly substantial working relationship has already been established.

Business Entertainment. Of course, business entertainment can have several different purposes. Business lunches can be used to hammer out a deal, conduct more relaxed and thorough discussions, or serve as get-acquainted sessions. Business dinners with spouses tend to be more formal affairs at which business is not the main point of conversation. Business can be discussed but not in such a way that it distracts from the enjoyment of the evening. In the old days, the men would retire and smoke cigars, drink brandy, and chew over a business deal. Today, a saleswoman is as likely to encourage her husband to talk to the client's wife, so she can have a quiet, businesslike word with him. Fortunately, cigars are out of style (many women, and some men, still find them offensive), but everyone who wants it is permitted to drink brandy!

In any case, business entertainment should be appropriate in cost and presentation. Important clients rate relatively expensive dinners with dancing or a show afterward. Business lunches should be confined to your client's status and your entertainment budget. You would not take any client to a fast food restaurant, nor would you take a client who spends only $100 a year on your products to a four-star restaurant.

Which type and place is appropriate for business entertainment depends entirely on each situation. Also, make sure your choice of entertainment appeals to your clients. You would hardly take a Methodist lay preacher to a Las Vegas-style review, but you need to know the subtle things about your client's preferences in food and dining establishment. For example, has your client ever eaten Japanese food? If so, does he like it; if not, is he adventurous and would he like to try it? Does his adventurousness in eating reflect a willingness to take a risk, or does he simply like raw fish? In business entertaining, if you follow the client's lead, you will do better than if you present unusual or daring alternatives. When in doubt, err on the side of conservatism. Except, perhaps, if you're in fashion, advertising, or entertainment.

EXPAND YOUR OPPORTUNITIES TO SERVE

Finally, cultivating clients enables you to discover new opportunities to sell, that is, to cross-sell your client on other products and services. However, approach cross-selling very carefully. Make new proposals or offers to clients *only* when you and your client identify a clear need, agree on the solution to that need, establish the anticipated benefits, and reach a consensus. Otherwise, if you badger a client about buying something new every time you call, he will feel put upon and abused.

Of course, every current client provides an opportunity to sell more. This situation makes cross-selling such an attractive alternative to making cold calls. And you can make the opportunity worthwhile when you identify clearly *complementary* products and how they will benefit your client *before* you suggest them. For example, an insurance salesperson made an initial sale of a small life insurance policy to a couple who had just begun a new business. The more he considered the situation, and the more successful the two became, the more he realized they could benefit from additional insurance services. And he knew that as an independent agent, he could find very reasonably priced policies.

During his next two cultivation calls, he suggested his clients examine two more types of insurance: business contents and an umbrella policy. The latter would protect the couple from any disastrous liabilities, i.e., a business customer falling down and breaking his neck in their establishment; the former would protect their investment in business equipment, although at the time, it was only a few business machines and typewriters. The couple considered the costs—somewhat more than they wanted to spend at the time, but they *could* do it—

and the benefits—relief from fear of significant loss and from heaps of trouble if there were a burglary or accident. They chose the relief and reassurance, and, it turns out, wisely. Through an unfortunate office building fire, they desperately needed the business contents policy, which they had even more fortunately increased two years after the first policy was written and a year before the fire occurred—all at the salesman's suggestion, which he made because he noted the rise in their prosperity and the increase in their equipment base.

CEMENT THE BOND

These small cross-sold policies helped cement the bond between the couple and the salesperson. The relationship developed into a more personal one as well, with business lunches, dinners at the couple's home, and occasional exchanges of gifts. And it continued for years after the couple moved the business to a different state because they knew that person would work in their interest in whatever way his professional involvement allowed him to do. The same principles apply whether you sell ice to Eskimos or semiconductors to the Japanese.

What should you know and do to cross-sell effectively? You should cultivate:

1. Wide knowledge of your products and services, but far more importantly, information about how they complement each other.

2. Continuously updated information about each client's situation.

3. Enhanced presentation and listening skills so you can more readily separate the wheat of the client's real needs from the chaff of a confused point of view.

4. Knowledge and use of the best available sales aids and tools, including automated client management systems, to allow you to readily identify potential client requirements and your complementary products.

5. An excellent working relationship with your own sales support staff and any in-house departments directly involved in satisfying your clients' requirements. Clients want action, not excuses, when something goes wrong, and you must know how to get your support team into action in the quickest, most effective way.

If you look at tremendously and consistently successful companies such as IBM, Delta Airlines, Exxon, many major insurance companies, AT&T, Hewlett-Packard, and many more, they all emphasize client cultivation, often to incredible extremes. IBM's large computer customers have been known to walk into their offices in the morning and find six-inch thick analyses of their information processing needs for the next decade. Of course, it was prepared by their sales rep courtesy of IBM.

These successful companies will spend great amounts of resources and even lose profits on any one sale to make sure they solve the client's problem as quickly as feasible. They do whatever is necessary to show their clients they care and to maintain a healthy long-term relationship, which they know will be profitable in the long run, if not in every single instance.

This willingness to take the extra step, to constantly look for opportunities to serve their customers, separates those who sell easily and well from those who do not. It is the real secret behind IBM's total domination of 70 percent of the information processing departments in Fortune 2000 corporations, the *crème de la crème* of income and profits in the computer industry. It is the real secret of consultative selling.

WEAVING A SUCCESSFUL CAREER IN CONSULTATIVE SALES

The new era of consultative selling is, in many ways, a child of the more complex, more rapidly changing and more competitive business climate of the 1980s. In a simpler time, clients often felt they could cope with gradual change, and didn't need any continual assistance from their vendors. Today, their attitudes have changed because the world has changed. Clients truly need continuing, yet evolving, relationships with salespeople based on servicing their needs. By the same token, you, the seller, are seeking new ways to make available a broader range of company products and services. In short, when margins on the goods you sell are buffeted by competition, you need new ways to make your company's products stand out from the rest. The services you make available by using consultative selling methods can provide the competitive edge you need.

Thus, consultative selling is not the old, simple progression from contacting the buyer to closing the deal, with delivery left up to someone else. In consultative sales, you may even be called upon to supervise delivery of the product, help install it and train employees in its use. Consultative sales, in fact, requires an intricate weave of related factors and skills which result in an attractive, resilient and high quality fabric. To summarize, these key factors and skills are:

- *Product knowledge.* First and foremost, you must know your products, their features, and their potential benefits for your customers.
- *Client needs.* You must discover and keep foremost in your mind your client's perceived and real needs.
- *Self-knowledge.* You must understand your strengths and weaknesses, and take advantage of the former while you take steps to remedy the latter. But always in the front of your mind should be ways you can best present both to serve your clients and customers.
- *Long-term objectives.* You must see that consultative selling is not usually a one-shot sale. More often, successful consultative selling rests on your understanding that you, your company, and your clients will derive the greatest satisfaction from a mutually beneficial long-term relationship.

Are there any rules by which you can keep these factors in your mind? Yes. They are the following.

1. Keep the sales triumvirate always together in your mind—your client, your company's product, and you.

2. Study—thoroughly and constantly—your products, and the improvements or modifications made to them.

3. Know exactly what your company's mission is, that is, if your company's corporate aim is to sell and service standard widgets, do not sell or service custom-made widgets, however tempting the market may be.

4. Keep a flexible frame of mind so you can determine how to turn your in-depth product knowledge into benefits and new applications for your customers.

5. Prequalify your sales calls and potential customers with a well-organized analysis procedure.

6. Learn your clients' true needs with careful probing and by empathizing with their situation, ratifying their success, recognizing their contributions, and respecting their knowledge.

7. Learn how to handle objections by cushioning your response and marshalling proof that your product or service will fulfill the client's need.

8. Maintain an adequate balance of service and profit. This may seem a company-wide problem, but for you it means using your only nonrenewable asset—your time—wisely and carefully. Balance the time spent providing consultative services with the anticipated level of profit. But always go the extra mile to fulfill your clients' needs when the occasion demands it.

9. Learn ways to measure the results—the real income—you and your company derive from the services provided.

10. Remember, when all is said and done, consultative selling, like any selling, depends on you and your enthusiasm, interest, honesty, and personal power. Cultivate and use them all.

Chapter 9

WIN, WIN, WIN —
BUT
WISELY

*Three
Consultative
Case Studies*

Following are three case studies. They are the actual practices of three companies, the names and precise businesses of which have been changed to protect their unique positions in each of their industries. The first case study is that of a company in traditional, "smokestack" manufacturing. The second is that of a unique service industry. The third is a case study of a high-tech reseller-service outfit.

In each case study, you will hear from a sales manager who is in charge of implementing consultative selling techniques in his company; each of these men has been a field salesman and, in fact, still is. Their comments will help you and your sales manager understand and use consultative selling.

CASE STUDY NO. 1:
BORN TO WIN = TRAINED TO SELL

Steven Gallo, Ph.D., holds three truths to be self-evident. The first is this: "The methods of the past are not good enough to be successful tomorrow." By this, he means that the end is near for formula selling, the standardized spiel that began with an opening, raced through a demonstration, and rolled over objections, questions—everything—to a closing, whether it worked or not.

Remember the stories about the vacuum salesman who strewed filth on the customer's rug? Then, the vacuum-man proceeded to a demonstration (luckily, most of them got most of it up), and finished with a bang-up closing: "Madam, can you afford to be without this wonderful machine?" That leading question begged for, and got, some doozies of answers. And not many sales.

"This sort of selling really won't work in today's environment," Gallo adds. "Not when you have long-standing relationships with clients."

As Director of Sales Training for a major national floor-coverings company, Gallo has brought this message to the company's hundreds of salesmen and women, with excellent results. So excellent, in fact, that his program—allied with four other corporate changes—reduced sales force turnover from 50 percent to 15 percent. (The other changes involved compensation, territories, and the like.) Needless to say, the salespeople who stay are happy and productive—and have become the professionals Gallo believes they must be to do the job.

THE GENETICS VS. ENVIRONMENT DEBATE: ARE SALES PROFESSIONALS BORN OR MADE?

Gallo's second truth is that, as they say in real estate, "Million dollar salesmen are not born, but trained." In essence, real estate discovered early what more and more industries are coming to realize. Only a few can be born snake oil salesmen—whom no one buys from nowadays anyway—but virtually any intelligent person can be trained to use consultative selling in some context; it is a mixture of technique, interest in the product and customer, and simple courtesy.

"In our company, we found that consultative selling is really a method in which the seller uncovers the needs of the customer," says Gallo, calling for the salesperson not only to present but to accept, as well. "Then, of course, the salesperson points out how the benefits of the product being sold can satisfy those needs."

Finding the client's needs, however, does not always depend on direct interaction, especially at the start, Gallo says. "For instance, if I were an independent training consultant, and I wanted to call on G.E. or General Motors, I would first try to see a catalog of the training courses they offer presently. I might notice there was no course in recruitment." That would be a place to begin. He could then, he says, make a preliminary list of questions to ask the contact he speaks with, including of course, whether they were aware of the absence of such a course. If they were not aware of the lack, then Gallo had already done them a valuable service he could follow up on. If they were aware, Gallo would do his best to find out why it existed—possibly for some very good corporate reason—before making a presentation and suggesting that they add his. Ignorance, in consultative selling, is never bliss.

THE WINNING EDGE

This, of course, is part of Gallo's third truth. Says he, "I sincerely believe that the most powerful competitive edge a company can have is competent, skilled people."

His company, which instituted a training program among five significant changes it has made recently, has a multistep training process for sales personnel, all the objectives of which are designed to make them competent consultative salespeople.

Their salespeople, once hired, are sent to the field and trained by their district managers. While each manager has his or her own style, tested at the home office mainly to help them enhance their strengths and counter their weaknesses, the training itself is self-paced by the trainee. But it follows specific modules, with testing for competence accompanying each. And, once a year, all "new hires" report to headquarters for two weeks of review, more training, and to see how the products they sell are made as well as how the company operates. "This information is vital," says Gallo, "although it may seldom be used *as is*. It is the depth of background that enhances a consultative selling approach; it means the salesperson really does know what he's talking about in terms of product."

A SEVEN-POINT APPROACH

Basically, this company's approach to consultative selling consists of seven components. They are:

1. Know the market.
2. Know the product.
3. Know all the product's features.
4. Know the benefits.
5. Know how to prove benefits.
6. Know how to ask questions.
7. Know how to handle objections.

PREMARKET ANALYSIS

"When I tell people they have to *know the market,* which they can do by making a market survey of their area, they think it's a big deal. But it's not. It can be as simple as surveying the neighborhood visually. What sort of homes are there? Is it a mid-town area, where installation is likely to be a larger factor than in a suburban do-it-yourself locale? Is it rural? Rustic? Does the neighborhood have architect-designed homes? Apartment houses? Tract homes? Housing projects? Is it in an industrial sector? What sort of location does the client's store occupy? Lots of floor space? And so on," Gallo says.

"We even suggest that the salesperson go into each store before trying to call on the owner, and see what the physical setup of the store is. It will save making up your mind to sell a large display to an owner who is pressed for floor-space.

"In short, you've got to get a feel for what the retailer is trying to do, and come up with some good solid suggestions you can offer him to help him do it better."

PRODUCT KNOWLEDGE

Says Gallo, "We expect our salespeople to have M.D.'s in the product, *to know the product* inside and out, what it does and why." This is essential, too, and can only be learned by study. But that study can include comments from people who have used it. It can include tips from other salespeople and managers on innovative uses for a product. It can include your own *bona fide* experience with a product.

KNOW THE FEATURES

Knowing all the product's features is based on knowing the total product itself. But it should be much more; it should include any special incentives for a merchant, whether in financial or special aspects of the product which appeal to a certain portion of a merchant's market. This gives you the opportunity to make suggestions that will be of value to your client.

KNOW THE BENEFITS

Knowing the benefits, Gallo emphasizes, means knowing what the product will do for the customer. At his company, this is a dual-level job. Because the firm sells to retailers, its own sales force must be completely familiar with what the product will do for the merchant. But, because the merchant is interested in his customer, the consumer, he will ask questions regarding its end-use, so the salesperson must be prepared to cope with that as well.

Your product might take up less space than a competing product—it might last a long time—it might make a home look like a palace or a bowling alley. Obviously, the benefits you stress will relate to the information you gleaned from your pre-market survey. You might want to emphasize the bowling-alley benefit to, for instance, someone serving a trendy, high-tech clientele interested in architectural minimalism. You would emphasize the palace line to more conservative store owners in more conservative locations, where the consumers are more traditional in their tastes, where a couple's home is their castle.

PROVE THE BENEFITS

If you *know how to prove the benefits* of your product, you can take advantage of a far less crude and far more sophisticated and meaningful successor to spreading dirt on a carpet to sell vacuums.

"We don't believe in pie-in-the-sky proofs; that's part of canned selling. Instead we offer data. For example, for one high-end line of floor coverings, we have a tracking system so that we can actually tell the storeowner what sort of profits it has made for people in similar situations," Gallo notes. "Beyond that, we can often put him in touch with a noncompeting merchant who has decided to carry the same line. We show clients letters from third parties. We rely on government reports, and often, media coverage in which our products have been favorably reviewed. By having all this material at your disposal, and by putting it at the merchant's, you are acknowledging that he is an intelligent buyer, and showing that you are an intelligent seller. In that way, it's a more equal basis through which to come to an agreement that benefits you both."

HOW TO ASK QUESTIONS

If you *know how to ask questions,* you'll find a blunt approach rarely works. More often, discretion is called for. "The salesperson must overcome his or her own personality and respond to the customer's," says Gallo.

Crudely put questions—"Do you sincerely want to be a millionaire?"—don't work much magic anymore, he notes. Still, there are many things you can discover through questioning, if your questions are intelligently based on your market survey. "How much would it mean to you to gain five square feet of selling space?" for example. If your client tells you that he moves $10,000 worth of product per square foot, it's logical that that space could mean $50,000. Can you supply a display that gives him that much more space than what he now has? If so, you've not only found out what he needs, but you're on your way to rounding up the proofs that will convince him to buy.

Basically, your questions should not be designed as lead-ins to a pitch—"Wouldn't you like to own this lovely car?" They should seek to truly elicit information that will help you help the client. Keep in mind, says Gallo, the old proverb of journalism, the five W's and an H: ask who, what, why, where, when—and how.

HOW TO HANDLE CONCERNS

In formula selling, handling objections often meant pretending not to hear them, answering them with an irrelevant claim, dismissing them with a wave of the hand. In consultative selling, it's much more important than that, and takes more thought to handle. *To know how to handle CONCERNS,* not avoid them, is a key difference.

"Obviously, the first thing to do is to listen," says Gallo. "Then, instead of offering a countermove, agree. We call this cushioning the response. You might say, 'Yes, I know exactly how you feel. Many of the other retailers I know felt the same way. But we've found that, once you've got the unit installed, rather than spending money on it, it will actually make money for you. Here's how.'" And then, says Gallo, you marshal "proofs."

USE THE "FEEL, FELT, FOUND" PATH TO SUCCESS

Most people, he adds, are eager to listen to suggestions and proofs, as long as they "feel" that you've got their interests firmly in sight. As for the above, Gallo says that the shorthand for it—and an easy way to remember it—is to call it the "feel, felt, found" method:

Here's how Gallo teaches his salespeople to respond:

Merchant: I *feel* that it's too expensive for me (or too big, or too green, and so on).

You: I know how you feel. Others have *felt* that way too.

You: But we've *found* that this is the way it works.

Further, says Gallo, there are only three categories into which the overwhelming bulk of concerns falls. They are:

- *Price* (too high)
- *Risk* (too great)
- *Inertia*

When you encounter these, you can use the feel, felt, found method to counter them, rather than using coercion. "In any case, besides the fact that coercion no longer works—if it ever really did—I think it's unethical," Gallo adds.

But it is not unethical to point out facts. For instance, if your merchant's objections are based on high price, show him that the price may appear high, indeed, but that the benefits to him support it.

Gallo explains, "Let's say we've suggested the Duke of Norfolk Portfolio of Floors, based on the merchant's basically affluent and design-conscious clientele. But he says the display costs too much. So we calculate X dollars per month, and compare that to the figures for increased income. With this product line, we can do that, as it has been tracked, and we have industry averages to use. It's not inconceivable that, for example, another $20,000 in gross income a year could be meaningful to the merchant. If this is what we come up with, based on the facts, we let him know. We're still not coercing him, merely giving him facts on which he can base an informed decision."

Through all consultative selling, Gallo says, he tries to do one thing: Move through *communication* to *rapport*, until his *recommendations* are accepted.

AVOID GLAD-HANDING

Although consultative selling is based on a long-term relationship, Gallo's company does not recommend that its salespeople just drop by and see clients. "We always go there to actually do something for them," Gallo says. "A cup of coffee is usually just a waste of everyone's time. If I'm taking him or her to lunch, that's fine. There is time to build rapport, and there is a trade of value. If I stop by the store, I don't just chat; I make sure the displays are full of samples and in good condition, I drop off updates for a display and try to be actively helpful. I even check on the store's inventory, if one is kept, and the merchant finds it a useful service."

CASE STUDY NO. 2:
BALANCED OUTPUT AND INCOME—THE KEY
TO PROFITABLE CONSULTATIVE SELLING

When Interworld Travel-Force Services, Inc. got its start, its executives knew it had to invest heavily in technology to deliver its basic services to its clients. It is one of the very few full-service corporate travel management companies; its technology had to enable it to book reservations on airlines and trains, for cars and hotel rooms, instantaneously. But the company's business isn't technology; it is service.

Selling a service, especially when it's new or complicated and takes a good deal of explaining, means you must begin as Interworld did, by doing two important things, says Sales Vice-President Arnold Dunns: (1) define your market, and (2) understand it.

DEFINE TO SUCCEED

"We first had to define our market. In our case, that's commercial travel, which is a far different sort of business than leisure travel.

"Second, we had to define the scope of our sales effort, and this we do using local information from our 600 sales organizations nation- and worldwide." In other words, management uses its own consultative sales force to consult with, as well. It's a slightly different twist on Gallo's program of sales force market surveys. And it means that the sales force must be consulting in the field.

As a new type of service business in a deregulated and increasingly competitive marketplace, Interworld provides a clear look at how "pure" consultative selling works and offers valuable advice to other, more traditional service industries such as banking and brokering, which are beginning to think about consultative selling.

UNDERSTAND YOUR MARKET NICHE, AND SELL TO IT

Next, they designed the product. "We first developed our concept of total business travel management. It's not just a frivolous luxury for corporations that can afford to have their executives pampered. Far from it. It is a service that can contribute directly to our client's profitability." Travel, he notes, constitutes the second or third largest line items of the budgets of Fortune 1000 companies. Thus, saving on this figure is of major concern to them.

Because Interworld is a service, says Dunns, "we sell by a process similar to that used by accountants, relocation management companies, legal offices, and so on. In fact, we begin with *education* of the client base, not sales," Dunns says.

To do this, the company, through its semiautonomous local offices, sponsors seminars and luncheon meetings, and other forums in which the message can be presented.

BOOST THE BENEFITS OF A NEW BUSINESS

"Our sales force must first generate forums in which they can talk about the evolution of travel management as a new industry. We point out that, until now, companies with no corporate travel department could end up going to every mom and pop shop in town to fulfill their executives' travel requirements. But, unless they worked out a specific commission-splitting agreement with the agent, they didn't save any money."

And, even corporate travel departments often had to deal through a variety of small agents, coordinating travel plans as they went along.

Says Dunns, "The benefit of taking the time to explain our industry is this: The clients and potential clients are made aware that there is now competition in the travel services, from the deregulated airline fares to hotel bookings. This is relatively new. Secondly, we teach them that they can, through us, take advantage of that competition to reduce their own expenditures and get not equal, but better, service."

USE FORUMS FOR DISCUSSION

Dunns says that none of Interworld's hundreds of representatives is given to pie-in-the-sky presentations. "It stands to reason that if we gather people for a seminar, they'll feel they're wasting their valuable time unless we tell them something that has substance. Far from intriguing people, we'll get a completely negative reaction."

Further, in order to use a seminar or symposium as a sales tool, says Dunns, "we must have programs, and the ability to perform in an aggressive, modern, and efficient manner."

Most of Interworld's salespeople have come to their positions either from the travel industry or from marketing management. So, many of them are experts already in presentation. Nonetheless, Interworld offers courses at headquarters in making presentations to groups, and provides not only brochures, but films to help the sales force make professional-looking presentations.

KNOW WHICH BENEFITS COUNT

If they have gotten their message across in a seminar or lunch meeting, says Dunns, typically the corporations they've presold in this way will call in several other single source suppliers before giving away their business.

"Strangely enough, at this point it's not always the service issues that count. Cost analysis is the only area in which many corporations feel secure in making a decision, so we must be prepared to give them one that meets their requirement," adds Dunns. This is just the opposite of Gallo's finding; his company manufactures and sells tangibles, so the added value of service is important to their clients.

The fact that buyers of tangibles want to see intangibles, and buyers of intangibles want to see something they can chew on is not surprising. It is merely the proof that buyers are getting sophisticated.

"Our prospective clients hear from our competitors that they can save 1 or 2 or even 4 percent in commissions by having them handle the corporate travel arrangements. But we point out that we are talking about greater figures than that. Even those savings, while considerable in most travel budgets, in no way offset the savings realized through proper management," Dunns says.

MAKE UP THE PROPER MIX OF
SERVICE AND PROFIT

One of the issues Interworld salespeople avoid, that is common to the travel industry, is the possibility of offering more services than you can be adequately compensated for. This is a valuable lesson for anyone in consultative selling whose income and profit nonetheless depend on commissions.

Says Dunns, "Travel agents still mainly make their profit from the commission paid to them by the airline or hotel and so on. It's possible to do so much work for a client that the commission isn't even adequate to cover our time, much less make a profit." By selling as Interworld does, on a fee-for-management basis, they have a structure in which they know it's possible to fully serve the client, and also meet sales and corporate expectations.

"This works, too, because part of our sales philosophy

includes selling the client not what is most profitable for us, but what he really needs," Dunns says. In virtually all corporations, this will consist of: economy, expertise (getting the travelers where they want to go, how they want to go), and the ability for the client to change plans mid-trip. This, particularly, is where the concept of travel management is valuable. "Our salespeople hit hard the fact that we have a twenty-four-hour telephone number clients can call and have their travel plans changed for them immediately."

YOUR PROFITABILITY—MEASURE RESULTS

How can Interworld tell if its educational approach to sales is working? Easily, says Dunns. "After the seminar the sales manager sponsors—or luncheon or symposium—he or she simply notes who of those attending called for further details or a consultation or proposal. Further down the road, they can add up the sales totals, and subtract the cost of the presentation."

When all is said and done in this service business, the key to profitable consultative selling for Interworld is offering a careful balance of services rendered for fees charged. But Interworld salespeople make doubly sure that the services provided are the services needed, a guiding principle any salesperson—in a service, marketing, or manufacturing company—can easily apply as well.

CASE STUDY NO. 3:
KEY WORDS AND KEY CONCEPTS UNLOCK
SALES PERFORMANCE

At InsuranceMate Computing, Inc., a growing, young company based in Hartford's central business district, the sales force is not expected to sell the product and services to customers; they are expected to "engage in consultative sales." Semantics? Yes, unless they're followed up by action, as they are here.

David A. Commager, vice-president, marketing and sales, is able to give the sales force grounding in the consultation concept that comes from the very top. Company founder Buckley C. Dolan decreed early in the company's growth that even the pricing of goods and services—which consists of business personal computing equipment and services—be "consultative." Thus, they sell no $3,995 computers; they may sell a package of computing equipment, services, and consultation for $4,500.

Agrees Commager, "In consultative sales, we are not dealing with the 'buy now before the special bargain is over' plan of action." In fact, this key factor, he says, is one of the main ways to differentiate consultative selling from the "hard sell." "Probably lots of people will disagree with me," he adds. "But in point of fact, closing a sale—any sale, consultative or 'hard sell'—is much the same except for this type of 'buy now' pressure and perhaps the wording of how you ask for the order."

KEYS TO PROSPECTING

All that, of course, is of primary importance to learning the philosophy of a consultative sale. But chronologically, it's not first. What's first, says Commager, is training. "We don't have any truly novice salespeople at InsuranceMate. All of them are experienced in sales. But what we have is a force of specialists in the industries we see as our target markets. For example, we have a force of twenty-five; these are divided into teams, including insurance, investment banking, commercial banking, management consulting, Big Eight accounting, manufacturing, scientifics, and consumer goods and services. Members of each team have, as well as sales knowledge and computing knowledge, a background in the target field."

TELEMARKETING

"Each Monday evening, all the members of all the teams meet, and we have a training session. Often, this session includes the planning of a Telemarketing Day." In traditional hard sell, this might have been a Morale Breakfast, at which "prospecting" goals were set. But the InsuranceMate concept includes much more.

"Let's say we decide on an area of an industry that we want to target. Our goal will be, at the end of the telemarketing day, to have set up ten *qualified* appointments. At the meeting, which is both fresh training and continuing training, we discuss exactly how that is to be done."

First, of course, the sales force is told what a "qualified" appointment *is*. Says Commager:

- There must be a reasonable probability that the company you contact will have a need or use for your product.
- There must be a reasonable probability that you are contacting the right person—the person with both the authority to make the purchase, and the budget to pay for it.
- There must be a reasonable probability that we have the systems and services to fulfill the client's requirements.

All this is determined by asking, but not simply by "digging around." Says Commager, the salespeople cover seven areas in depth before they pick up the phone. They are:

1. Who am I calling?
2. Why?
3. When am I going to call?
4. What is my *main message* for this person?
5. What, exactly, will I say?
6. How is the contact likely to respond?
7. What are the questions I can use to gather further information from him or her prior to asking for an appointment?

In all of this, from targeting to contacting, Commager says that four factors are paramount. "You must be strong, clear, concise, and honest." Why? There are many personal, corporate, and moral reasons, naturally. But, he adds, there's a purely practical one, as well, for keeping even small bits of "fudging" off the phone. "The telephone is not an effective instrument for throwing bull. You can't feign knowledge over the phone; you've no body language to use to make a point. The inflection in your voice isn't enough."

TELECHARTING

While the *telemarketing* is in progress, says Commager, the salespeople track themselves and their original thoughts about the possibilities for objections. "We use a *telechart,* which is just eight letter-size sheets taped together, with categories typed on them for objections and responses."

The categories include, among others:

- *Money objections* (discount asked for, too expensive)
- *Literature* ("Don't come see me, send me a booklet")
- *Nonspecific* ("I'm too busy")
- *Using a competitor's products and services*

Naturally, all of Commager's salespeople phrase their responses to these objections in their own way. But, consultative selling or not, Commager insists that they be not only smart, but persistent. "For myself—and I hope my sales force—the only thing that makes me hang up the phone with a thank you and no further effort is when I hear this from a contact: 'My company just went into Chapter 11 bankruptcy proceedings.'" Says Commager, he's only heard that about twice over the years.

LOCK UP KEY CONCEPTS TO LOG ON TARGET

Before InsuranceMate salespeople go into the field to fulfill the appointments they have set up, they review the company's mission. "InsuranceMate is a market-driven firm which offers highest quality personal computer-based products and services which increase productivity and creativity of managers and professionals engaged in analysis and decision making." Quite a mouthful, but they don't have to retell it to clients that way.

"What we are aiming for is basically product knowledge. It's easy to define what we do if a client says, 'I've got a need for a metal stress-testing computer. Can you do that?' The answer is clearly 'No.'

"But what if I'm selling to a Big Eight accounting firm, and my contact tells me he has a new spreadsheet package that doesn't do what he wants, and asks me to enhance it? It may sound like our business. We do support systems for accounting firms. But I still know, based on my knowledge not only of our product but of our mission, that that is not our business. We don't sell or modify machines or programs. We meet client requirements in 'decision support' which means a blend of interactive computation and judgment. We seek out, advise about, sell, deliver, and support hardware, peripherals, and software. We assist managers and professionals in three key aspects of business problem solving: modeling and numerical analysis, data retrieval and management, and communications.

"Trouble in sales and follow-up typically begins," he says, "when your reach exceeds your grasp."

THE SELLING GROUND: KNOW THE TERRAIN

"The ideal situation, when you do get in to see the client, is for him or her to instantly order forty PCs, ten printers, sixteen modems, a service contract, a subscription to InsuranceMate *On-Line Ideas* publications, all right there. But, because our company is market-driven and applications-driven, it is more typical that the client, after meeting with the salesperson, asks for a proposal of hardware, software, and support that would perform his tasks," says Commager.

"For this, the salesperson returns to the office, possibly asks a colleague if he or she has had a similar case and what the solutions were, or goes to our Research and Development Department for help."

Once the proposal is worked out, the client and salesperson have one more chance to take either of two paths. "It's ideal, and more frequent I'm happy to say, when the client bases his or her decision on our reputation and goes ahead with the agreement. But sometimes, they ask for a demonstration, and we gladly provide it." The more successful and honest the demonstrations that InsuranceMate provides, of course, the more solid their reputation becomes, obviating the need for demos.

CROSS THE GAP FROM CONSULTING TO SELLING

"Possibly because so many people in consultative sales were consultants *per se,* many don't do well at closing. But it is a necessary part of selling. Luckily, there are really only two to learn, the conditional closing and the assumed closing," Commager says.

"The conditional closing goes like this: 'If I can demonstrate to you that proceeding on our proposal will generate more income, save time, and result in sounder decisions, when will you be ready to begin installation?'

"The assumed closing consists of something like this: 'Now that you've seen how well this can work for you, why don't you start by putting PCs into the Finance Department first?'

"A third closing would be the time-dependent closing, which is useful in the hard sell, but almost never appears in consultative sales. In fact, for consultative sales, the conditional closing is most common. It's knowledge-based, but certainly, it is a closing, and the salesperson must get to it."

AFTER CLOSING

When does the salesperson stop being the contact in consultative sales? Almost never. For instance, Commager says his salespeople periodically contact their existing clients—an easy maneuver in a growing field like high-tech where everyone knows changes are frequent and often of great benefit. Specifically, InsuranceMate salespeople can contact their clients to offer:

- A new training course InsuranceMate has developed
- A new product InsuranceMate R and D has tested and recommends for the client's applications
- A new InsuranceMate service or support arrangement
- On-site service and maintenance.

"Amazingly enough, in consultative sales, our clients often contact us, often before delivery of their purchase is complete," Commager explains. "What we've sold them is specifically tailored to their needs, and it's likely that their needs will change over time. Typically, too, if what we've sold does do what it is intended to, they'll outgrow its capabilities in a short time and will contact us for updates."

FINE POINTS

It's obvious that InsuranceMate takes pains with its product, image, and marketing. Likewise, says Commager, they want their sales force not only to sell, but to reflect well on the company. In consultative sales, it's impossible to divorce the product from the company providing it, and the company from the people who make it up. Those who would succeed understand and depend on a well-forged partnership.

BIBLIOGRAPHY

Edwards, Betty, *Drawing on the Right Side of the Brain*. Los Angeles: J.P. Tarcher, Inc., 1979.

Girard, Joe, *How to Sell Yourself*. New York: Warner Books, 1981.

Henley, Nancy M., *Body Politics: Power, Sex and Nonverbal Communication*. Englewood Cliffs, NJ: Prentice-Hall, Inc., 1977.

Johnson, Spencer, M.D., and Larry Wilson, *The One Minute Salesperson*. New York: William Morrow and Company, Inc., 1984.

LaBella, Arleen and Dolores Leach, *Personal Power: The Guide for Today's Working Woman*. Boulder, CO: Newview Press, 1983.

LeBouef, Michael, *Working Smart: How to Accomplish More in Half the Time*. New York: Warner Books, 1979.

Molloy, John T., *Molloy's Live for Success*. New York: Bantam Books, 1981.

Nierenberg, Gerard I., *Fundamentals of Negotiating*. New York: Hawthorn Books, 1973.

Nierenberg, Gerard I. and Henry H. Calero, *How to Read a Person Like a Book and What to Do About It*. New York: Cornerstone Library, 1971.

Patton, Forrest H., *The Psychology of Closing Sales*. Englewood Cliffs, NJ: Prentice-Hall, Inc., 1983.

Peters, Thomas J. and Robert H. Waterman, Jr., *In Search of Excellence: Lessons from America's Best-Run Companies*. New York: Warner Books, 1982.

Richardson, Linda, *Bankers in the Selling Role: A Consultative Guide to Cross-Selling Financial Services*. New York: John Wiley & Sons, 1981.

Vipperman, Carol and Barbara Mueller, *Solutions to Sales Problems: A Guide for Professional Saleswomen.* Englewood Cliffs, NJ: Prentice-Hall, Inc., 1983.

Waitley, Denis, *10 Seeds of Greatness: The Ten Best-Kept Secrets of Total Success.* Old Tappan, NJ: Fleming H. Revell Company, 1983.

INDEX

A

Alternatives close, 150
Assumptive close, 148

B

"Big picture" approach, 122–124
  advantages of, 123–124
  questions in, 122
  responses to client, 122–123
  tactical selling and, 123
Buyer profile, guidelines in creation of,
  35–36
Buying signals, 143–147
  negative, 145–146
  physical, 144–147
  positive, 146–147
  verbal, 143–144

C

Clarifying probes
  examples of use, 68–69, 74–75
  purpose of, 66
Client management software,
  54–58
  features of, 55
  Sales Edge®, The, 57
  Saleseye®, 57
  Sales Manager®, 56
  Sell!Sell!Sell!®, 56–57
Closed-ended questions, 65–66
Closing a sale, 135–153
  alternatives close, 150
  assumptive close, 148

Closing a sale (*cont.*)
  buying signals, 143–147
    negative, 145–146
    physical, 144–147
    positive, 146–147
    verbal, 143–144
  fear close, 152–153
  fear of closing
    fear of rejection, 139–142
    fear of success, 138–139
    overcoming, 136–137
  "give in" close, 152
  "hook" close, 151
  ignorance involved in, 137–138
  impassive close, 151
  and lack of faith in product, 142
  "ours versus theirs" close, 150–151
  presentation close, 149
  pressure factors, 137
  straightforward close, 153
  stumbling block close, 149
  succession close, 149–150
  summary close, 153
  testimonial close, 148–149
Company profile, guidelines in creation
  of, 32–35
Competition, knowledge about, 16–18
Consensus
  process of, 131–132
  statements/questions by seller, 132
Consultation protocol
  and commercial sales, 40–41
  creation of, 38–39
  value of, 40
Consultative presentation
  asking for sale, 22